24

OCR HISTORY A

The German Reformation 1517–55

Alastair Armstrong | Series editors: Martin Collier | Rosemary Rees

This book is to be returned on or before the last date stamped below.

– 9 JAN 2012

WITHDRAWN FROM STOCK

www.heinemann.co.uk

✓ Free online support
✓ Useful weblinks
✓ 24 hour online ordering

01865 888080

Official Publisher Partnership

Heinemann is an imprint of Pearson Education Limited, a company incorporated in England and Wales, having its registered office at Edinburgh Gate, Harlow, Essex, CM20 2JE. Registered company number: 872828

www.heinemann.co.uk

Heinemann is a registered trademark of Pearson Education Ltd

First published 2008

12 11 10 09 08
10 9 8 7 6 5 4 3 2 1

British Library Cataloguing in Publication Data is available from the British Library on request.

ISBN 978 0 435312 61 9

Typeset by TechType
Original illustrations © Pearson Education Ltd 2008
Illustrated by TechType
Cover design by Pearson Education Ltd
Cover illustration: Luther at the Diet of Worms © akg-images
Edited by Kirsty Taylor
Index compiled by Eleanor Holme
Printed in the UK by Henry Ling Ltd

Acknowledgements
The author and publisher would like to thank the following individuals and organisations for permission to reproduce photographs:

Galleria degli Uffizi, Florence, Italy/The Bridgeman Art Library: p. 3; akg-images: p. 4; Getty Images: p. 11; Mary Evans Picture Library: p. 16; Visual Arts Library (London)/ Alamy: p. 26; akg-images: p. 31; akg-images: p. 43; Getty Images: p. 49; akg-images: p. 56; akg-images: p. 59; akg-images: p. 62; akg-images: p. 86; akg-images: p.96

Written sources
p. 91 Source E: Geoffrey Woodward, The Sixteenth Century Reformation. Hodder 2001. Reproduced by permission of John Murray (Publishers) Ltd.

Every effort has been made to contact copyright holders of material reproduced in this book. Any omissions will be rectified in subsequent printings if notice is given to the publishers.

Dedication
To my Mother and Father

CONTENTS

HOW TO USE THIS BOOK

The aim of this book is to give a comprehensive explanation of all the events of the German Reformation. The emphasis of this examination unit is on historical enquiry. However, before students can engage in meaningful historical enquiry, they need to have a full understanding of the relevant events, issues and controversies. The book therefore follows a chronological order and outlines in detail the key issues and core content as specified by OCR.

Key Issue 1: What were Luther's main ideas and how and to whom did they spread?
This is covered throughout much of the book, particularly chapters 2 and 3.

Key Issue 2: How did the authorities react to Luther from 1517 to 1521?
This key issue is covered in chapter 2.

Key Issue 3: What was the impact of Lutheranism in Germany from 1517 to 1530?
This is covered throughout much of the book, particularly chapters 3 and 5.

Key Issue 4: Why did Lutheranism survive in Germany between 1530 and 1555?
This key issue is the focus of chapter 4.

Features
There are many features in the margins of the book which are directly linked to the text and will help stimulate the students' imagination and pick out key information.
Key Terms – these pick out and define key words.
Key People – these give a brief biography of important people.

Key Ideas – these pick out important ideas, either of the time or of historians studying this period.
Key Events – these give a brief overview of important events.
Key Themes – these pick out important themes of the period. This feature is also used to highlight sections of the text which are particularly relevant to a Key Issue.

Skills

Students will be given an opportunity to develop skills as they progress through the book through the source analysis activities at the end of each chapter.

An overview of the skills required and how these can be developed from students' GCSE skills are explained in detail in the *Planning and Delivery Resource* (see below).

Exam Café

There are Enquiry style activities at the end of each chapter to help candidates to build up the necessary source analysis skills as well as knowledge of the period.

The text in the book is supplemented by an exciting **Exam Café** feature. The Exam Café is split into three areas: Relax, Refresh, Result!

- **Relax** is a place for students to share revision tips.
- **Refresh** your memory is an area for revising content.
- **Result** provides examiner's tips and sample answers with comments.

Planning and Delivery Resource

The German Reformation chapter of this resource contains guidance and advice for ways to approach and teach this topic for the OCR specification. There are student worksheets which help to build up source skills for the examination requirements. This also contains lots of additional source material and an Exam Café with more tips, sample answers and detailed examiner commentary.

INTRODUCTION

By 1555 the religious landscape in Germany had been irreversibly altered by the actions of Martin Luther and his followers. In 1500 the Catholic Church had been one of the institutions which bound German society together. Yet as a consequence of the Peace of Augsburg in 1555, the foundations had been laid for a Germany whose inhabitants could choose between Catholic and Protestant faiths. Clearly it is important that we understand the role of the Catholic Church in society and the anticlerical attitude which prevailed over much of Germany and some other parts of Europe in 1517. Reformers and humanists had challenged the doctrine of the Catholic Church before Luther came along, but none of them gave birth to a significant movement. Therefore we must examine not only the individuals but also the environment in which they operated if we are to explain the success of Lutheranism in Germany. Moreover, it will also be important to identify the limitations of Lutheranism, and chart its relatively conservative progress after 1530 in the hands of the princes. By 1555 Lutheranism had failed to live up to its early promise in terms of territorial expansion. Indeed, Lutheranism had not spread with any success beyond the frontiers of Germany and Scandinavia. Having said that, Luther's challenge to the medieval Catholic Church left an indelible impact on the social, political and of course religious map of Europe. Other Protestant churches, such as that of Calvin, evolved and developed during the course of the second half of the sixteenth century, creating further unrest and lasting change.

CHAPTER 1

What was the nature of the Pre-Reformation Church in Germany?

KEY TERMS

The Pope in Rome The Catholic Church regards the Pope as the successor of St Peter (head of the Apostles) and, as such, he has full and supreme power of jurisdiction over the Church in matters of faith and discipline. Indeed, the Pope is regarded as infallible on most matters of faith and morals. That is to say that any doctrinal decision he makes is binding on the whole Church. The Pope is elected by a college of cardinals and sits at the top of a strict hierarchy consisting of cardinals, archbishops, bishops and priests. During the early modern period, the Pope had great political power and influence, in part as a consequence of the Papal States in Italy over which he ruled.

Primer A primer was a devotional book that included the psalms and the litany of saints. Dating back to the fourteenth century, primers were often seen as religious textbooks to teach and instruct children and adults alike.

Abuses should be seen as the corrupt practices of the Catholic clergy. An example of an abuse might be the buying or selling of a clerical post or title, a practice known as simony.

INTRODUCTION

In 1500 there was only one faith in Western Europe, namely Catholicism. At the head of the Catholic Church was the **Pope residing in Rome**. The Church played a central role in the lives of ordinary people. Their loyalty and devotion can be seen in the large amounts of money left to the Church in wills or the considerable sale of **primers** and prayer books. However, one must be careful not to generalise and, in some parts of Europe during the early sixteenth century, the Church was seen to be failing in its spiritual duties. **Abuses** were prevalent within the late medieval Catholic Church, although the extent of corruption varied from region to region. It might also be added that such abuses had been taking place for decades and were nothing new. It is therefore crucial to take a close look at the state of the Church before the Reformation in order to understand why Martin Luther became such a significant figure in European history.

HOW WAS GERMANY GOVERNED IN 1500?

Across Europe the Catholic Church was a very powerful institution, not only in religious terms but also politically and militarily. In kingdoms such as France and Spain rulers took steps to guard the independence of their churches from Rome, giving themselves rights to appoint bishops and collect taxes. The Pope remained the spiritual head of the Church, but his political influence was curbed by such measures. In Germany the political environment was more decentralised, which made it easier for the papacy to intervene in religious and political affairs. One key reason why Luther was so successful in challenging the power of Rome in Germany was a growing dissatisfaction with the papal exploitation of German lands. Luther was also fortunate that the political landscape of Germany was favourable, and he gained important and influential supporters from amongst the nobility.

It is crucial, therefore, that we examine how Germany was governed in the 1500s, and the role of the Church within that structure:

- The Holy Roman Empire comprised over 350 semi-autonomous states, part of which were German lands. Germany as a nation state did not exist in the sixteenth century.
- In theory these lands were ruled by the Holy Roman Emperor. Since 1440, only members of the House of Habsburg had been elected Emperors. In practice, real power lay with the princes or bishops who ruled over each state. This arrangement suited both parties nicely. The Habsburgs gained the prestige that came with the grand title of Holy Roman Emperor while the princes were able to protect their territorial rights and privileges without disrupting the balance of power.
- The seven leading princes of the Empire were known as Electors, as they alone had the right to vote for a new Emperor. They were the Elector of the Palatinate, the Electors of Saxony and Brandenburg, the Archbishop Electors of Mainz, Trier and Cologne, and the King of Bohemia. Some of these princes, such as the Archbishop Elector of Mainz, ruled over both Church and state giving them enormous power in their locality.
- Within the Holy Roman Empire there were eighty-five Imperial Free Cities which were not ruled by princes. Some of these cities, such as Augsburg and Nuremberg, were centres of trade, and all of them guarded their independence fiercely.
- There was an imperial Parliament of sorts called the Diet, at which supposedly binding decisions were made for the whole of the Empire. In practice, the princes and representatives of the cities who attended the Diet often returned to their respective states and continued to act independently and look after their own interests.

Conclusion

The power of the Emperor within the Holy Roman Empire was weak, and political influence rested predominantly with the princes. The fact that Habsburg power was so diluted helped Luther when it became clear that some of the princes supported his movement in the late 1520s.

WAS THE PRE-REFORMATION CHURCH IN GOOD HEALTH?

It is possible to outline two interpretations of the state of the Catholic Church on the eve of the Reformation.

- One interpretation views the Catholic Church as being on the brink of collapse: a Church so riddled with abuses and corruption that it could no longer cater for the spiritual needs of the people. In short, a Church in need of reform but incapable of or unwilling to reform from within its own structure. This line of argument certainly has its advantages in that it neatly explains **Martin Luther**'s success: a German reformer faces an inadequate Catholic Church.

Martin Luther by Lucas Cranach the Elder.

However, history is rarely that straightforward.

- A second line of argument presents the Catholic Church in a relatively healthy state: a Church that generally fulfilled the needs of the people and operated effectively despite isolated cases of ill behaviour and ignorance among the clergy; a Church linked to the people socially, religiously and economically. In short, a thriving Church.

As is so often the case, the historian must look to find a middle ground on this issue. Undoubtedly, the corruption of the Catholic Church has been exaggerated in the past. However, one thing is clear: by 1555, the Holy Roman Empire was bi-confessional (two faiths were being practised: Catholicism and Lutherism). From a religious perspective, the old belief of 'one faith, one law and one king' no longer rang true. Martin Luther and his ideas were a success in many parts of Germany and, by the end of the sixteenth century, Protestantism had spread in some form or another to most corners of western Europe. Challenges to the teachings and structure of the Catholic Church had, in the past, come from men such as **Jan Hus**, the Bohemian reformer, but had always ended in failure. For Luther to be a success, the circumstances in Germany

Jan Hus preaching. German engraving c.1850.

had to be favourable and, in that part of Europe, the Catholic Church cannot have been as healthy as in others. It is clear, therefore, that the Catholic Church continued to operate effectively in some areas, while in others it was stagnant and in need of reform.

THE POSITION OF THE CATHOLIC CHURCH IN SOCIETY

For the people of late medieval Europe, religion was of great importance. The Church played a central role in their lives, not just spiritually but also socially and economically. There were few non-believers in the practices and teachings of Catholicism. People generally believed that the Church provided all the right answers and that it was only through the Catholic Church that salvation could be attained. The people were linked to the Church in various ways.

- **Spiritually**, through the seven sacraments and the road to salvation. The seven sacraments (listed on page 6) were seen as a way of participating in the mystery of Christ through symbolic actions. Salvation was regarded as the deliverance from sin and admission into heaven brought about by Christ. The fear of what awaited them after death was a very real one for early modern people, and the wish to attain salvation and enter heaven often guided their actions on earth.
- **Economically**, through taxation, the upkeep of the Church, and wills.
- **Socially**, through active participation in festivals and processions.
- **Pastorally**, through confession, penance and the cult of saints. Confession was a practice for early modern Catholics, during which the participant would acknowledge his sins to a priest. In order to make up or atone for sins that had been committed, penance often had to be carried out. Penance might be regarded as a form of punishment for sins that had been committed and, depending on how serious the transgression had been, the form of punishment varied from fasts and the carrying out of pilgrimages, to flogging and imprisonment. Yet absolution from one's sins was crucial

to the laity, as many feared dying and suffering for unatoned sins.

- The cult of saints was the practice of worshipping the remains of saints. Saints were seen as being close to God and capable of communicating with God on our behalf: therefore, through the saints, divine power could be accessed. Often, the laity picked out particular saints to worship, believing them to be capable of looking after their interests and protecting them from evil. Reformers such as Luther condemned the worshipping of saints because, for them, such practice blurred the unique status of Christ.
- **Educationally**, through the learning of doctrine. Doctrine can be regarded as a principle of religious belief. Such theology was taught to children and adults through Church services, primers and catechisms. A catechism was a comprehensive account of Catholic doctrine, including the Apostles' Creed, Ten Commandments, Lord's Prayer and the Seven Sacraments. However, one should not forget that the Bible was in Latin, an edition known as the Vulgate which had been translated by St Jerome, and was therefore inaccessible to the majority of the laity.
- **Politically**, through the activities and policies of the local bishop.

The Sacraments

Unquestionably, the most important link between the Catholic Church and the people was the spiritual one. For the people of late medieval Europe, the path to salvation and heaven was found by following the teachings of the Church and this meant following the seven sacraments:

1 Baptism
2 Eucharist
3 Penance
4 Confirmation
5 Matrimony
6 Extreme Unction
7 Ordination

Catholic Mass The Mass refers to the prayers and ceremonies that make up the service of the Eucharist. It is important to recognise that the ordinary people might attend mass on a regular basis but only take communion (or Eucharist) once a year. The Mass and Communion are the visible bond between people, priest, and bishop, who are all one body who share the one bread.

Eucharist The Eucharist was a sacrament and miracle celebrating Christ's sacrifice and the Cross. The priest would consecrate the bread and wine at the altar, and they would then become the body and blood of Christ.

Transubstantiation is the Catholic belief that in the Mass, the bread and the wine were entirely transformed miraculously into the body and blood of Christ.

The Eucharist

Of these seven sacraments, it was the **Mass**, or celebration of the **Eucharist**, that was of crucial importance to Catholics. While a person was baptised only once, married once and died once, the hearing of Mass was a weekly, if not daily, event. By attending Mass, the people were recognising the visual embodiment of Christ and celebrating his ascension to heaven. The Catholic understanding of the Mass was based around **transubstantiation**. This idea was, and is, at the heart of Catholicism. In the Mass, the priest will bless or consecrate the bread and wine as part of the service. Through this process, Catholics believe that the consecrated elements of the bread and wine are transformed into the actual body and blood of Christ. One cannot underestimate how powerful this service was. The people truly believed that to celebrate the Mass was to witness a miracle and that it was only through attending Mass that salvation could be reached. It is unlikely that the ordinary people would understand the whispered Latin verse of the priest, yet they did understand the significance of the ritual.

Penance and sin

Also important to the belief of Catholics was, and is, the idea of sin. A sin is committing an offence against God. One could not receive the Eucharist in sin unless one repented (admitted guilt) and confessed one's sins. Repentance was therefore of great importance, especially because death was a major concern for the people of late medieval Europe (not surprising, given the regular outbreaks of war, plague and famine). Every Catholic wanted to be prepared for death, to have repented of sin before entering heaven. Catholics believed that to enter purgatory (the place in which souls were cleansed before entering heaven) would result in considerable suffering for the individual. This issue was a preoccupation of Catholics, and they had a number of strategies for dealing with it. However, the vast majority of the laity actually took communion (participated in the taking of bread and wine) only once a year – at Easter.

- Prayers and Masses for the dead were said in order to release loved ones from purgatory.

- Religious guilds existed in which lay people (non-priests) could say prayers and Masses for the dead.
- One's own time in purgatory might be reduced through the purchase of indulgences. Indulgences were pieces of parchment sold by the clergy and signed by the Pope offering a general pardon for sin and thereby releasing the faithful from purgatory. One can see why indulgences were a highly attractive proposition.

Participation

In general, religion in late medieval Europe was about participation and activity.

- Feast days and saints' days: Religious processions and pilgrimages to local shrines were popular, while feast days and saints' days attracted large crowds and were observed universally by the people. For example, thousands of pilgrims flocked to Wilsnack in northern Germany over the course of the fifteenth century to witness the miraculous bleeding hosts there. The town became wealthy on the back of the cult of the Precious Blood and soon Wilsnack was home to a very grand church. The church was a most important social centre for the people – a natural gathering point in what was predominantly a rural society.
- The decoration of churches: The loyalty and devotion of the people can be seen first through the building and decoration of churches. For example, the German village of Balgach had a newly built chapel in 1424. The money to build and adorn such churches came from the villagers themselves. This financial commitment came out of either a genuine devotion or merely from the hope that salvation might be attained through such good deeds. Yet the sheer number of **roods** surely illustrates a devotion to Christ, while the reliance upon saints throughout Europe indicates more than merely a **pragmatic** attachment to Catholicism. Indeed, images and paintings of saints were commonplace in the churches of Europe.
- Devotion to saints: There was a widespread belief that miracles were performed at the shrines of saints, and most people adopted a saint who they believed looked after them through curing illness or protecting crops.

Saints were influential in the world of sixteenth-century Germany, and some represented particular causes. Rupert of Bingen, for example, was believed to protect pilgrims on their travels. In a period of great uncertainty, religion brought stability and solace. The most popular image was that of Our Lady, Mary, mother of Jesus. Throughout Europe, people paid for her image to beam down from windows or to inspire through statues. Even after death, men and women would leave money to pay for candles to be lit before their favourite saint. Churchwardens' accounts from across Europe reveal the amount of money contributed by a community towards the upkeep, maintenance and expansion of churches during this period. Ornately gilded churches, glitteringly adorned with figures of saints, were in some ways testament to the devotion of the people.

- Relics: Most people believed in the power and importance of religious relics. Holy relics, such as thorns from the crown of Christ or splinters from the True Cross, were bought or venerated (worshipped). Pilgrims travelled hundreds of miles to view and touch such holy relics. Sceptics noted enough nails from the True Cross to make thousands of crosses, yet for the vast majority of believers such ideas did not cross their mind. They were content with what the Church had provided.

- Financial payments: Large amounts of money were left in wills to the Church and the laity also regularly paid taxes to the Church, often in the form of the tithe, which amounted to a tenth of all income and produce. Moreover, mortuary dues (money paid when people died), the Peter's Pence (a tax payable to the papacy) and the buying of indulgences represent other economic links between the laity and the Church. The taxes were regularly paid with little resentment.

All of the above suggest that, on the eve of the Reformation, the Catholic Church was in a strong and healthy state. Indeed, in many ways, it was the unifying bond of the community.

WHY WAS THE CATHOLIC CHURCH IN NEED OF REFORM?

Despite the strength of the Catholic Church explained above, there were aspects of the Church that had fallen into disrepair. This was noticeable across Europe, particularly in some of the German states. Corruption and abuse of position as a member of the Church was not uncommon among the higher ranks of the Catholic clergy. Such corruption existed at the very top.

The problems of the Papacy

Even the Pope in Rome hardly set a fine example. In 1500 the papacy was a powerful institution politically and spiritually. The Pope was generally Italian and, although technically an elected position, it had become dominated through bribery by aristocratic Italian families such as the Medicis. Furthermore, a papal schism (split) in the fourteenth century (1309–77) had resulted in two popes, one based in Avignon the other in Rome. Although this was resolved by the beginning of the fifteenth century, successive popes seemed to care more about wealth and prestige than spiritual leadership.

Top of most historians' lists of badly behaved popes comes Alexander VI (1431–1503). Formerly Rodrigo Borgia, Alexander VI was made a cardinal by his uncle, Pope Calixtus III in 1455, before becoming Pope himself in 1492 on the death of Innocent VIII. It was widely recognised that Alexander owed his position to the widespread bribery of the College of Cardinals. Although Alexander started brightly by restoring order in Rome and challenging the authority of the Italian princes, he soon held a string of mistresses and fathered a number of illegitimate children, most of whom were looked after with clerical titles and income. In total, Alexander appointed 47 cardinals, including his teenage son Cesare. The luxury of the Alexandrian papal court knew no bounds while, as a patron of the arts, Alexander grew in stature, even commissioning Michelangelo to draw up plans for the rebuilding of St Peter's Basilica in Rome. Political manoeuvring and the furthering of his family were more important to Alexander than spiritual matters although, in

**Girolamo Savonarola
(1452–98)** was a religious
and political reformer in Italy
in the fifteenth century. He
argued in favour of a moral
reform of the Church. In
Florence he insisted that
gambling was forbidden and
all costly clothes burned.
However, Savonarola claimed
he was a prophet and this led
him into conflict with the
Church. In 1498 he was
executed, hanged and burned.

Habsburg–Valois Conflict
Between the years 1521 and
1559, the royal houses of
Habsburg and Valois were in
conflict, with the chief
protagonists in this struggle
being Charles V, Holy Roman
Emperor and Francis I, King
of France. These two men
were primarily fighting over
dynastic claims and in
particular the dominion of
Italy. The significance of the
conflict with regard to the
Reformation was that,
initially, Pope Leo X
(1513–21) resented Habsburg
intrusion into Italy and
attempted to prevent Charles
from becoming Emperor. In
the long term, it took the
attention of Charles V away
from Germany, and Francis I,
despite being Catholic, offered
military and financial aid to
the German Protestants in
order to disadvantage Charles.

1498, he did oversee the burning of **Girolamo Savonarola**, who had been convicted of denying papal authority and preaching heretical doctrine. In 1503, Alexander died when he accidentally took poison at a dinner party hosted by Cardinal de Corneto. The poison had been intended for the host! Julius II (1503–13), the Warrior Pope, cared more about preserving his position in Europe amid aggression from France and the Empire, while his successor Leo X (1513–21) was obsessed with the building of the grandest church in Christendom, St Peter's Basilica in Rome.

Contemporary drawing of Pope Leo X (1513–21) by Sebastiano del Piombo.

During the sixteenth century, the Pope's position in central Italy came increasingly under threat from the **Habsburg** and **Valois** expansions. Therefore, in order to strengthen his defences, the Pope looked to exploit the wealth of his subjects. Increased taxation and dispensations for marriage, as well as the sale of offices, all contributed to the wealth of the Curia (see page 44). Indeed, it was the decentralised and easily exploitable German states that Rome looked to exploit most keenly.

The papacy could extract large sums of money from German nobles when they wished to purchase Church positions for their younger sons. The scope for financial gain was great, as nearly one fifth of Germany was under the control of semi-independent archbishops and bishops. Clerical office brought prestige and political power. At the highest end of the spectrum were the posts of the spiritual electors of Mainz, Trier and Cologne, but there were also hundreds of other lucrative positions within the Church which could be sold. Younger sons barred from inheritance rights could be set up for life. If they were still under-age, a further papal dispensation could be purchased allowing them to take up office immediately. Additionally, papal dispensations could be purchased allowing for more than one clerical office to be held at the same time. Only the Pope had the power to issue such exemptions from normal Church laws. Over the course of the fifteenth century there is evidence to suggest that the papacy withdrew large amounts of money from the German states. Princes also benefited from papal ambition, as demonstrated when Eugenius IV (1383–1447) attained princely support by allowing the collection of papal taxes for a period of time, which more or less amounts to an act of bribery.

Bishops and clergy

Furthermore, there was some evidence that such abuses filtered down into the ranks of the clergy. Complaints against archbishops, bishops and priests were various, such as:

- Simony: the buying or selling of a benefice.
- Nepotism: the securing of a benefice or post for one's family.
- Pluralism: the holding of more than one benefice at the same time.
- Absenteeism: the inability to be present in one's benefice in order to look after one's flock.
- Clerical marriage: priests were not allowed to marry and they were ordered to take a vow of celibacy. Yet many were unable to stick to their vows and gave in to lustful desires. Some clergy had mistresses and often bishops would maintain illegitimate children by providing them with positions in the Church.
- Illiteracy: ignorance of the Old and New Testaments and consequent inability to spiritually administer to their flock.

The picture thus described is of a clergy that had lost its true sense of vocation, and ensuing resentment from the masses would seem inevitable. Yet, while such corruption did make the Church more vulnerable to attack in some areas, these abuses were exceptional and not necessarily widespread. However, given a certain set of circumstances, such low moral standards could certainly promote support for relatively radical reform.

WHO HAD PREVIOUSLY CHALLENGED THE AUTHORITY OF THE CHURCH?

Jan Hus

Few had attempted to challenge the 'one true faith' because to do so might lead to a charge of heresy, and to be found guilty of such a crime would mean death, usually by fire. Yet some celebrated examples do exist. One such man was Jan Hus (1369–1415; see page 4), who was burned alive on the order of the Pope because of his heretical views. Hus criticised the Catholic practice of communion, asserting that both the laity and the clergy should receive the bread and the wine, rather than the laity receiving only the bread. He also attacked the corrupt nature of the Church and the supreme authority of the Pope. Hus was summoned before Pope John XXIII at the Council of Constance in 1415 and, on refusing to recant his views, was found guilty of heresy. He was executed in 1415, as was his companion John of Prague the following year. Yet after his death, a small group of followers known as Hussites existed, and fought in the name of their reformer until the mid-seventeenth century.

Hus, like his fellow reformer in England, John Wyclif (1320–84), is often seen as a precursor of Luther. Both challenged the authority of the Catholic Church and both advanced the idea that the **Holy Scriptures** were the only valid source of truth and authority. Wyclif even undertook an early translation of the **Bible into English**. As such, Luther's subsequent translation of the Bible into German echoes the actions of Wyclif over a century before. The point here is that Luther's ideas were not new. One key factor, however, sets Luther apart. Hus and Wyclif both led popular movements (Hussites and Lollards), but neither was able to form a rival Church in the way that Luther did, suggesting once again that Germany at the beginning of the sixteenth century presented a specific set of conditions that allowed Lutheranism to develop.

The Holy Scriptures were the written word of God as outlined in the Old and New Testaments. For Christian humanists such as Erasmus, the problem with the Latin translations and the work of Church fathers such as Jerome, Origen and Augustine was that they were deemed to be inaccurate and, over time, had been misinterpreted. Humanists spent much time editing New Testaments, translating and writing biblical commentaries. For reformers such as Luther, the words and substance of the scriptures became the crux of Protestant calls for reform.

Bible in English Although the Lollards undertook early translations of the Bible, the first translation from Greek into English to be published was by William Tyndale (1494–1536) in 1525. Tyndale's debt to Wyclif was enormous.

GERMANY ON THE EVE OF THE REFORMATION

The success of Luther in Germany was in no way predictable. There remains much evidence to suggest that German people were tied to the beliefs and rituals of the Catholic Church. Participation in pilgrimages, unstinting devotion to saints and the popularity of devotional literature such as Thomas a Kempis' *The Imitation of Christ* all show that loyalty to the Catholic Church remained high. There was no tradition of dissent in Germany, and there had been no heresy trials since the 1470s. To argue that Luther based his success on a growing sense of anticlericalism and discontent is therefore too simplistic.

That said there are some specific examples of an underlying resentment of Rome and of anticlerical sentiment which are worth noting, if only to suggest a sense of spiritual anxiety amongst the laity. One must also remember that this was a laity with growing expectations of the Church resulting from increased access to education and increasing literacy rates. The clergy were often unable to meet such expectations.

- No other territory in Western Europe was exploited by the papacy to the extent that the German lands of the Holy Roman Empire were. Germany had no central authority to restrict papal authority. This meant that papal taxation was high, and the appointment of foreign nobles by Rome to German Sees was rife. Anti-papalism existed in Germany long before Luther.
- Over the course of the fifteenth century numerous proposals for the reform of the Church were put forward. For example, the *Reformatio Sigismundi* (c.1438) was a reform manifesto which attacked the greed of the papacy and the quality of the clergy. Grievances were also drawn up on a regular basis by the German Estates (made up of the princes), entitled *Grievances of the German Nation* and listing the abuses of the Church while highlighting the tyranny of Rome. Such agendas for change were largely limited to the literate elites.
- The peasantry in Germany felt the burden of clerical taxation most acutely. On top of rents and dues owed to

landlords, the clerical tax or tithe was an unwelcome imposition. In 1476 Hans Bohm, the so called Drummer of Niklashausen, incited radical revolution amongst the peasants in protest at noble and clerical oppression. Bohm proclaimed an apocalyptic message to his followers, predicting the end of the world and the Second Coming. He raised expectations of a just and equal society in which the common man would stand alone. Perhaps unsurprisingly, Bohm was burned as a heretic by the Bishop of Wurzburg. Still, there was an ingrained sense of injustice amongst the peasantry which carried through to Luther's arrival at Worms in 1521. En route to the Imperial Diet Luther was confronted by images of the Bundschuch, or clog, on the doors and walls of houses – a sign of peasant support for a man they believed might bring lasting change.

- Popular culture was steeped in mysticism and a belief in prophecy. Joachim of Fiore (1132–1202) was an Italian Cistercian monk who believed that he was living in the Age of the Son after the coming of Christ. He prophesied that at some time after his demise the Age of the Spirit would arrive. In the Age of the Spirit, the old order would die out and a period of spiritual renewal would begin, overseen by a monk like himself. Fiore's prophecies remained popular in Germany in the sixteenth century, and many viewed Luther as the prophet of renewal to herald Fiore's Age of the Spirit.

WHAT WAS THE IMPACT OF THE RENAISSANCE ON CATHOLICISM?

The **Renaissance** was important in the context of Church reform because it encouraged a new intellectual outlook and a re-examination of accepted ideas. The Renaissance fostered Christian humanism, an intellectual movement in which some important academics became preoccupied with studying, understanding and translating the original scriptures. Through this study of the original scriptures, it was believed that authoritative interpretations could be made and old mistranslations put right. Furthermore, this fresh outlook also involved discussion of a reform of the

Renaissance From the French meaning rebirth, the Renaissance is seen to centre around Italy, with the effects encompassing all of Europe. The period 1370–1527 is often deemed to be that in which literary and artistic talents such as Petrarch, Dante, Bruni and Boccaccio were allowed to flourish and a new wave of learning and thinking entered Europe. Whether such a period can actually be defined is a contentious issue, but the significance for the Reformation was that ancient, classical texts were re-evaluated and scripture re-translated. Also, Christian Humanism emerged from the literary and scholastic environment of the Renaissance.

practices of the clergy. Three men in particular are worth noting in any discussion on humanism.

- **Desiderius Erasmus (c.1466–1536).** The foremost humanist in Europe was Desiderius Erasmus, from Rotterdam. He talked about a restoration, by which he meant an improvement of Christianity through the translation and interpretation of sacred texts. Erasmus himself translated the New Testament into Greek in 1516 and into Latin in 1519. Although one would never label Erasmus as a revolutionary, there is little doubt that such translations paved the way for later German editions overseen by Luther. Moreover, moral criticism of the corrupt and worldly clergy from Erasmus in his *Praise of Folly* (1509) further weakened the Church. Erasmus, it must be stressed, was not like Hus or Wyclif. He did not propose a split from the Catholic Church and he was not opposing its fundamental doctrines. He was putting forward ideas to make people better Christians and to reform the Catholic Church from within. Indeed Erasmus demonstrated his conservatism when, after initially supporting the radical Luther, he then condemned him in his work of 1524 entitled *On*

Painting of Desiderius Erasmus by Hans Holbein the Younger, etched by Lefort.

KEY THEMES

Moral and Spiritual renewal based around Scripture Both Erasmus and Luther called for greater standards of education amongst the clergy and less worldly/material principles. *In Praise of Folly* and *Julius Exclusus* attack corruption and ignorance. This idea was popular at an academic level and may have filtered down to the masses but essentially Erasmus and More (*Utopia*) were scholars and academics working from within the boundaries of the Church. Luther was able to build on latent anticlericalism within Germany which had deep rooted social/economic origins.

Re-translation of the Scriptures The translation of the New Testament into Greek by Erasmus (1516) provides the basis for Luther's translation of the New Testament into German in 1521. Vernacular translations were more radical as they make the Word of God more accessible to the common people. The intellectual foundation of Lutheranism is clearly in evidence here. Luther would later use the authority of scripture to reinforce his doctrine (for example faith alone comes from Epistles to St Paul).

the Freedom of the Will. Luther responded with *De Servo Arbitro,* or *On the Bondage of the Will,* and the split was sealed.

- **Johannes Reuchlin (1455–1522)** was a German humanist trained in the law and noted for his exposition and understanding of Hebrew texts. His *De Arte Cabalistica* (1517) was seen as an important contribution to unravelling the ancient Jewish tradition of mystic interpretation of the Bible. Reuchlin was, until his death, a Roman Catholic, but the controversy caused by his work in Rome made him an intellectual forerunner for Luther and in some ways paved the way for the criticisms made by the Wittenberg reformer.

- **Ulrich von Hutten (1488–1523).** In Germany, humanists such as Ulrich von Hutten were to include a patriotic tone in their writings. He and others made clear their nationalist resentment of a foreign pope as is shown in von Hutten's work entitled *Vadiscus* (1520). It can be argued that von Hutten laid the foundations for Luther's challenge. Von Hutten even pledged military support for Luther in the early years of the movement, thus suggesting a more radical stance than Erasmus.

In some ways, these men – and perhaps especially Erasmus – were therefore academic forerunners to Luther, especially in their endorsement of original scripture. Yet they were no threat to the Catholic Church; indeed they were very much a part of it.

HOW FAR DID CHRISTIAN HUMANISM PAVE THE WAY FOR LUTHERANISM?

In some respects the Christian humanist movement did indeed lay the foundations for Lutheranism in two important respects. The Christian humanist calls for **moral and spiritual renewal** promoted **anticlericalism**, and the **re-translation of the Scriptures** provided a model for later vernacular efforts. However it is crucial that we understand the limitations to this argument. Most Christian humanists and certainly Erasmus were doctrinally and politically conservative. As Lutheranism showed its true colours after 1520, any sympathy from Erasmus disappeared. Added to this is the idea that Christian humanist thought was at a specifically academic level, whereas Lutheranism had developed into a genuinely popular movement by the 1520s.

Therefore Christian humanism is important in paving the way for Luther's more radical ideas, especially in the scriptural context. It is also important to remember that Luther's doctrine was not really original; Hus and Wyclif had both raised these ideas before, and were an important influence on Luther himself. There is no doubt that humanist activity made Luther's translations easier and showed him the influence of the printing press. Yet circumstance and the German environment would catapult Lutheranism beyond the scholarly boundaries of Christian humanism.

CONCLUSION

There is little evidence to suggest that the Church was becoming more unstable as it entered the sixteenth century.

- Corruption and abuse among the clergy had been occurring for centuries, and again it should be stressed that such behaviour was generally isolated and localised.
- In many ways, abuses among the higher echelons of the clergy were accepted as the norm.
- While the Church remained the single means of grace and salvation, it was becoming vulnerable.
- The Church had set itself on a pedestal by claiming to be the sole interpreter of the Bible, and the issue of papal supremacy also implied a special and superior status. Such authority was accepted by the masses in 1500. Yet just over half a century later the Holy Roman Empire would house two faiths.
- The challenge from Luther was a relatively radical one, which paid scant respect to existing Church laws and beliefs. Clearly the German environment, and in particular the anti-clerical sentiment which existed there, aided his struggle.

ACTIVITY

Below are some exam-style questions on this first chapter. Please note that you will not be asked questions in the OCR examination on the period before 1517 but it is important to understand the background to the events of the Reformation. These first activities give you an opportunity to discover the types of questions that you will find in the examination. Help and advice on answering exam questions as well as sample student answers are available in the Exam Café section from page 109.

The Pre-Reformation Church

(a) Study Sources A and D

Compare these Sources as evidence of opposition towards clerical wealth.

(b) Study all the Sources

Use your own knowledge to assess how far the Sources support the interpretation that people were dissatisfied with the Church in the Holy Roman Empire on the eve of the Reformation.

Source A: The *Reformatio Sigismundi* was written in c.1438, but published between 1476 and 1522.

Take a good look at how bishops act nowadays. They make war and cause unrest in the world; they behave like secular lords, which is, of course, what they are. And the money for this comes from pious donations that ought to go to honest parish work, and not to be spent on war.

It seems to me that great evils have arisen in the western part of Christendom since the Pope imposed the rule of celibacy. It may be a good thing for a man to keep himself pure, but observe the wickedness now going on in the Church! Many priests have lost their livings because of women. All the hatred existing between priests and laymen is due to this.

Reformatio Sigismundi, c.1438

Source B: This account lists the grievances of the Craft Guilds of Cologne, 1513.

Clerical persons should from now on bear the same civic burdens as burghers. Let the clergy pay taxes on the wine they tap for themselves. The Council should instruct the preachers of the four regular orders to preach nothing but the true word of God and to utter no lies or fables.

The Craft Guilds of Cologne, 1513

Source C: This account is written by an early supporter of Luther.

Johann Tetzel, a preacher of indulgences in Germany, raised an enormous amount of money which was then sent to Rome. His indulgences were so highly prized that, when he entered a town, the papal authorisation for the indulgences was carried on gold cloth. All the priests, monks, members of the town council, men, women and children met him in a solemn procession. All the bells were rung and all the organs played. Even God himself could not have been welcomed and entertained with more honour. We Germans are fools to be robbed in this way.

Friedrich Myconius, 1519

Source D: From a letter from Ulrich von Hutten to the Elector of Saxony.

We see that there is no gold and almost no silver in our German land. What little may perhaps be left is drawn away daily by new schemes invented by the council of the most holy members of the Roman Curia. What is squeezed out of us is put to the most shameful uses. Leo X gives part of it to his nephews and relations. A portion is consumed by a host of most reverend cardinals and a variety of other officials forming the elite of the great head church.

Ulrich von Hutten, 1520

Source E: A present day historian comments on peoples' attitudes to the Church in the late medieval period.

Religious processions and pilgrimages to local shrines were popular, while feast days and saints' days attracted large crowds and were observed universally by the people, thousands of pilgrims flocked to Wilsnack in northern Germany over the course of the fifteenth century to witness the miraculous bleeding hosts there. The church was a most important social centre for the people – a natural gathering point in what was a predominantly rural society. The loyalty and devotion can also be seen through the building and decoration of churches. The German village of Balgach had a newly built chapel in 1424. The money came from the villagers themselves.

Alastair Armstrong, *The German Reformation*,
Heinemann, 2008

CHAPTER 2
What was the nature of Lutheranism?

LUTHER CHRONOLOGY

1483	Born the son of a copper-miner in Eisleben.
1501	Matriculates at the University of Erfurt where he reads liberal arts in preparation for a career in law.
1505	Struck by a bolt of lightning during a storm; a reputedly life-changing experience as Luther now commits himself to God, proclaiming to St Anne that he will become a monk.
1506	Takes the monastic vows of the Augustinian order.
1510	Visits Rome on behalf of the Augustinian friars and returns appalled with the worldly and material nature of the papacy.
1512	Receives a doctorate of theology from the University of Wittenberg.
1513–8	Lectures on Romans, Galatians and Hebrews to the students of Wittenberg, from which his views on the role of faith in salvation become clearer.
1517	Posts his Ninety-Five Theses on indulgences to the door of the Castle Church in Wittenberg.
1518	With the succession of Holy Roman Emperor Maximilian I under discussion, Frederick the Wise of Saxony gains Luther a hearing with Cardinal Cajetan in Augsburg rather than the papally preferred venue of Rome.
1519	Leipzig disputation with Johannes Eck.
1520	Leo X issues the bull *Exsurge Domine*, which provisionally excommunicates Luther from the Catholic Church.
1520	Luther has his three great works published, defining his doctrine and beliefs. *The Address to the Christian Nobility of the German Nation*, *The Liberty of a Christian Man* and *The Babylonish*

Captivity of the Church are regarded as Luther's three most important works.

1521 Condemned by the Emperor Charles V at the Diet of Worms and, by the resulting edict, he is proclaimed a heretic and his books are to be burned.

1521 Resides in Wartburg Castle where he translates the New Testament into German. Published in 1522, Luther continually revised it until his death. The translation of a readable and commonly accessible New Testament in the vernacular was crucially important to Lutheranism.

1521 The radical Andreas Karlstadt takes control in Wittenberg, celebrating the first evangelical communion and carrying out attacks on Catholic statues and images.

1522 Returns to Wittenberg and restores order with his Invocavit sermons.

1525 Marries Katherine Von Bora, a former nun whom he had helped to escape from Nimbschen Convent with eleven others in 1523.

1525 Peasants' Revolt erupts in southern Germany. Luther condemns the disorder in his tract *Against the murdering thieving hordes of the peasants*.

1525 Split with Erasmus complete after Luther writes *De Servo Arbitro*.

1526 Luther's German Mass completed providing for weekday services and doctrinal instruction.

1526 First Diet of Speyer.

1529 Large and small catechisms published in German, allowing the common man access to Lutheran doctrine.

1529 Second Diet of Speyer. Six princes and fourteen cities issues the Protestation.

1529 Marburg Colloquy with Zwingli results in failure to agree over the Eucharist.

1530 Diet of Augsburg and the Confession of Augsburg.

1536 Wittenberg Concord overseen by Bucer brings compromise between north and south Germany over the Eucharist.

1537	*Schmalkalden Articles* offer an overview of Lutheran theology and justify resistance to the emperor.
1541	First Colloquy of Regensburg.
1545	Council of Trent opens.
1546	Second Colloquy of Regensbug.
1546	Luther dies in Eisleben.
1547	A crushing victory for the Imperial forces over the League of Schmalkalden at Muhlberg.
1548	Augsburg Interim drawn up.
1552	Princely Revolt led by Maurice of Saxony.
1555	Peace of Augsburg.

MARTIN LUTHER: THE EARLY YEARS

In order to understand Martin Luther's challenge to the beliefs and rituals of Catholic Europe, one must recognise that Luther himself did not set out to lead a breakaway movement from the Catholic Church. Indeed, he had chosen to join the Augustinian religious order at Erfurt in 1505 as a novice monk and thereafter enter the priesthood in 1507. As a monk, he had decided to devote his life to God through prayer and contemplation. However, in 1510, Luther travelled to Rome, a visit that opened his eyes to certain aspects of the Catholic Church. When he returned to Germany he was transferred to the monastery at Wittenberg and made a professor at the university. There is little doubt that Luther was a troubled man during these early years in Wittenberg. Luther's problem was questioning the nature of Christianity, along with his relationship with and understanding of God. However, at Wittenberg, he met **Johannes von Staupitz**, an important member of the Augustinian order who helped him overcome his doubts and torment. The questions he asked went to the heart of the Catholic faith.

The path to salvation

Luther felt an overwhelming sense of guilt and inadequacy in trying to meet the demands of a perfect God. In short, Luther was highly sceptical of the Catholic Church's view that man could make himself acceptable to God through his own efforts. Good works alone seemed inadequate to Luther as the means of setting an individual on the road to salvation. This obviously contradicted the teaching of the

Catholic Church at the time. In attempting to discover the secrets of his religion, Luther turned to the Bible. From 1513, he undertook a study of the scriptures under the watchful eye of Johannes von Staupitz. He lectured at the university on sections of the Bible: in 1513 he lectured on the Psalms, in 1515 his lectures were on St Paul's Epistle to the Romans. Later, Romans 1:17 would lead Luther to recognise that God's justice did not consist of a demand but rather it was a gift given by God to humans and received through faith alone. Reading the Bible, preparing his lectures and discussing issues with von Staupitz led Luther to certain important conclusions.

Faith

For Luther, the most important revelation that came out of his studying the Bible was the importance of faith. The Epistles of St Paul revealed the key to his problems. The scriptures stated that God would extend mercy and salvation to all those who identified through faith with Jesus Christ. Luther came to believe that man never ceased to be a sinner before God. Christ was the only man who satisfied the demands of God. Therefore, in order for man to be saved and enter heaven, he had to put his trust in faith alone. The line in the Bible in the gospel according to St Paul read: 'the just shall live by faith' and from now on this idea was to form the crux of Luther's doctrine. The implications for the Catholic Church were serious.

Luther's ideas on faith and salvation undermined the role of good works, as they now became a sign of salvation rather than a cause. Furthermore, **indulgences** and the idea of purgatory were also under threat from a doctrine that stated that salvation was freely offered by God to all people.

In 1515, these radical teachings were causing a stir among the students and professors of Wittenberg University, and Luther showed no signs of letting up on his beliefs.

THE INDULGENCES AFFAIR

How did Indulgences work?

The doctrine of the Church stated that the pope had the power to forgive sins and release souls from purgatory. The

Pope was able to draw upon the Treasury of Merits which were the accumulated good works of saints which could be used to atone for the sins of man. These papal remissions of guilt could be purchased in the form of indulgences. In 1476 the Church changed its position on indulgences stating that they could be bought on behalf of dead relatives.

Why did Luther condemn the sale of indulgences?

Luther's condemnation of indulgences was based on the following objections:

- Sinners could not purchase forgiveness through indulgences as forgiveness came from God as a result of true repentance and contrition.
- The Church did not have the authority to issue indulgences, because only God granted forgiveness for sins.
- Even if the Pope did have the authority to free men from sin why did he charge money for it?

The arrival in Wittenberg in 1517 of **Johann Tetzel**, a Dominican indulgence-selling monk, prompted action

KEY PEOPLE

Johann Tetzel (1465–1519) Having studied at Leipzig, Tetzel quickly rose through the clerical ranks, being named inquisitor for Poland and later Saxony. In 1517, he preached indulgences for St Peter's in Juterborg and Zerbst, near Wittenberg, while serving the Archbishop of Mainz. Thus Tetzel came into contact with Luther and the indulgences affair sparked into life.

IOHANNES TETZELIUS, PIRNENSIS
MISNICUS, MONACHUS ORDINIS SANCTI DOMINICI
FRANCOFURTI AD ODERAM, PRÆCO, FORNICARIUS ET
NUNDINATOR, BULLARUM PAPALIUM
INDULGENTIARUM, Anno 1517.
Donatus d. 7 August. Anno 1519.

Johann Tetzel's Sale of Indulgences (contemporary handbill).

The son of Lorenzo de Medici, Leo was groomed for papal office from his days at university in Pisa. On becoming Pope in 1513 he sought to exclude foreign influences from Italy, while courting important monarchs such as Francis I. Indeed, Leo favoured either Francis or Frederick of Saxony succeeding Maximilian as Holy Roman Emperor, rather than another Habsburg in the form of Charles. However, the Imperial electors voted otherwise and Leo shortly had to turn his attentions to Luther. Notably in 1517, Leo X had to appoint 31 new cardinals after a plot to poison him was uncovered.

Luther's ideas expressed in the Ninety-Five Theses are important for **Key Issue 1** (see page iv).

from Luther. The ruler of Saxony, Frederick the Wise, had banned Tetzel from his lands, not on religious grounds, but because he wanted no competition for the funds that he raised through his impressive relic collection. That aside, people flocked from all over to buy Tetzel's indulgences.

Unbeknown to the ordinary folk, profits from the sale of the indulgences would go towards two enterprises. Some of the money went towards the building of St Peter's Basilica in Rome, whilst most of it went to Albert of Brandenburg, Prince-Archbishop of Mainz, so that he could repay the money he had spent bribing important clergymen and princes to elect him. This deal was approved of by **Pope Leo X**. Such justifications merely spurred Luther on to denounce indulgences with greater venom.

The Ninety-Five Theses

In autumn 1517, Luther read a copy of the *Instructio Summaria*, issued by the Archbishop of Mainz to guide indulgence sellers such as Tetzel. Indulgences were portrayed as a convenient way of absolving one's sins and reconciling oneself with God. Tetzel himself preached to the people that 'in these letters of indulgence all the ministries of Christ's passion are engraved and etched', while preachers were also encouraged to associate the coin falling into the money chest with the soul moving from purgatory into heaven. The rhyming couplet:

As soon as coin in coffer rings
The soul from purgatory springs,

illustrated this for the laity. Luther had already preached against the errors of selling indulgences and written a letter of complaint to the Archbishop of Mainz, so, when he decided to prompt an academic disputation on the matter, the content of the theses was already formulated in his mind. In the traditional fashion, Luther nailed his Ninety-Five Theses to the castle church door in October 1517, inviting those interested to discuss the matter. The theses outlined the way in which indulgences did not contribute to a good Christian life and indeed obscured the word of God. Below are some examples from the theses, which were originally written in Latin. Traditionally, the posting of Luther's

Ninety-Five Theses is seen as the beginning of the German Reformation. Of course, Luther had no idea that a popular movement would emerge from such criticisms.

Thesis 21

Hence those preachers of Indulgences are wrong when they say that a man is absolved and saved from every penalty by the Pope's Indulgences.

Thesis 27

It is mere human talk to preach that the soul flies out of purgatory immediately the money clinks in the collection box.

Commentary: Here, Luther is asserting that the Church has no real power over the souls of the dead in purgatory, while also referring to the aforementioned jingle.

Thesis 32

All those who believe themselves certain of salvation because of letters of pardon will be eternally damned together with their teachers.

Thesis 38

Yet the Pope's remission and dispensation are in no way to be despised for as already said they proclaim the divine remission.

Commentary: Luther here states that those lulled into believing that buying indulgences will bring salvation will themselves be damned. Also, he interestingly notes that indulgences are not to be totally dismissed as they do bring some solace to the weak and insecure.

Thesis 50

Christians should be taught that if the Pope knew the exactions of the preachers of Indulgences he would rather have the basilica of St Peter reduced to ashes than built with the skin, flesh and bones of his sheep.

Commentary: This shows a harsh and provocative attack on the corrupt practices of indulgence sellers.

Thesis 62

The true treasure of the Church is the holy Gospel of the glory and the grace of God.

Commentary: Luther extols the virtue of preaching the Gospel, the true word of God, which is in danger of being obscured by indulgences.

Thesis 86

Since the Pope's wealth is larger than that of the crassest Crassi of our time, why does he not build this one basilica of St Peter with his own money, rather than with that of his faithful poor?

Commentary: Although the theses were not meant for widespread circulation, one wonders if Luther knew that they might be circulated in German, for here is a point aimed directly at the common man, reinforcing widespread anticlerical sentiments.

Thesis 94

Christians should be exhorted to seek earnestly to follow Christ their Head through penalties, deaths and hells.

Commentary: Luther brings the theses to a close with a reiteration of the merits of true faith and repentance in attaining salvation.

The impact of the Ninety-Five Theses

Luther's purpose was not to rouse the people into revolt, but to prompt an academic debate on the essence of salvation and to make people aware that men such as the pope and the Archbishop of Mainz were endangering souls. Yet Luther was bound to bring attention to himself and, by the end of 1517, printed editions of his theses had reached Leipzig and Nuremberg. Shortly thereafter, Luther became famous throughout Germany. The angry reaction of the Archbishop and Tetzel merely helped to escalate the affair. Tetzel remarked that Luther would shortly be in flames while, in Frankfurt in January 1518, Dr Conrad Koch drew up retaliatory theses on behalf of Tetzel, repudiating the claims made by Luther. The undergraduates at Wittenberg burned 800 copies of the counter-theses. Meanwhile, Luther travelled to Heidelberg for a meeting of the **Augustinian order**, where he defended his theology for the first time outside Wittenberg. It became clear that the Catholic Church was going to have to deal with Luther.

What were Luther's intentions in October 1517?

Historians have given the Ninety-Five Theses a key place in the story of the early Reformation in Germany. Luther's action in nailing the theses to the door of Wittenberg's Castle Church has acquired iconic status. Even the date of 31st October has acquired significance, remembered as it is today as *Reformation Day*. Successive biographies of Luther have portrayed him as the heroic David, challenging the mighty Goliath in the form of the Catholic Church. Similarly most biographies of Luther take him at his word that he only intended for the Theses to spark academic debate rather than popular outcry. Yet historians have come to question Luther's intentions. Three possible aims exist for Luther in October 1517:

- The Ninety-Five Theses were sent privately in a letter to the Archbishop of Mainz to make him aware of the abuses that were being carried out in his name. Perhaps all Luther intended was for the Archbishop to step in and discipline Tetzel.
- The Ninety-Five Theses were posted on the Castle Church door in order to stimulate academic debate in

KEY TERMS

Augustinian order In 587 St Augustine was sent to England to reform the Church of England. He set up a monastery in Canterbury and was chosen to be the first archbishop. The order that followed the rules of St Augustine is known as the Augustinians.

Wittenberg. Did Luther merely want to encourage discussion on the issue of indulgences?

- The Ninety-Five Theses were meant to provoke a public outcry across Germany. Did Luther intend to undermine the Catholic Church on a grand scale?

Luther subsequently wrote that he had no intention of distributing the Theses across Germany and that matters were quickly taken out of his hands. The historian Michael Mullett takes issue with this claim, however, and argues that the Ninety Five Theses may have been drawn up with more than just academic debate in mind. He cites two key pieces of evidence:

1. Luther was sending copies of the Theses to people by 11th November 1517, knowing that his ideas were going out into the public domain and were likely to be published.

2. The language and tone of the Theses appear to have been styled in certain places to reach a popular audience. In some instances the Theses appears to be a practical teaching document in which Luther instructs the people in the Word of God. In one case he writes: 'When our Lord and Master, Jesus Christ, said Repent, he called for the entire life of believers to be one of penitence'.

What can the Ninety-Five Theses tell us about Luther in 1517?

Although history has defined Luther's actions in 1517 as the beginning of the Reformation it is important to remember that Luther still regarded himself as a loyal follower of the Roman Catholic Church. Luther condemns indulgences on the grounds that they were unnecessary for salvation. In his eyes sinners could win forgiveness by recognising and owning up to their own sins. True contrition and repentance from within would win forgiveness from God. The Luther of 1517 remained grounded in the doctrine of the Catholic Church. Whilst Luther launched a stinging attack on the sale of indulgences in 1517, his reasoning was by no means radical.

THE CATHOLIC REACTION

The response of Leo X

Whilst one might question Luther's intentions in 1517, the controversy was still interpreted by the Church as an academic, scholarly one and was treated as such by the Catholic authorities. Pope Leo X ordered Luther to travel to Rome in order to answer for his opinions and beliefs, an invitation he declined. Instead, the Pope sent an Italian representative, **Cardinal Cajetan**, to Germany. His task was to make Luther aware of the grave errors in his beliefs. Further to that he was to make clear the danger of expressing such opinions. In the eyes of the Catholic Church, Luther was implicitly denying papal supremacy and he had to be publicly reprimanded and made to see the error of his ways. Yet Rome was about to encounter, for the first time, the stubborn and courageous nature of Martin Luther.

What was the significance of Luther's meeting with Cajetan in 1518?

Cardinal Cajetan did meet Luther in October 1518 at Augsburg, but was far from successful in making him alter his opinions or recant. Cajetan's aim was to persuade Luther to take back his views on indulgences. However, Luther held firm, stating that unless his views could be

KEY ISSUES

The reaction of the papacy is important for **Key Issue 2** (see page iv).

KEY PEOPLE

Cardinal Cajetan (1469–1534) became a cardinal in 1517, having served as the official Dominican representative in Rome. Although Luther thought him 'as fit to deal with his case as an ass was to play the harp', Cajetan was actually able and wrote several tracts defending the papacy and various elements of Catholic doctrine. Neither was he a blinded bigot, even suggesting to Pope Clement VII in 1530 that communion in both kinds and clerical marriage should be conceded to the Protestants as a sign of compromise.

proven to be incorrect through scripture he would not change them. Luther's meeting with Cajetan reveals a number of key issues:

- The Ninety-Five Theses had clearly made the Catholic authorities aware of Luther and his ideas. He was perceived to be a threat but one which could be reasoned with and won back to the Catholic fold.
- Cajetan told Luther not to disturb the peace of the Church and reminded him of the danger of being labelled a heretic. This was the first time that Luther had been made to answer for his ideas to the authorities. He was being forced to compromise his views in order to maintain the unity of the Church. Yet Luther believed that what he had laid down in the Ninety-Five Theses was the truth as revealed in Scripture. He refused to deny that truth and even attacked the Pope's right to interpret Scripture.
- At the start of 1518, Luther seemed ready to see the error of his ways and convinced that he was still a loyal son of the Roman Church. By the end of 1518 Luther was becoming more assured of his doctrinal ideas and less willing to give in to Rome.
- Luther was also favoured by political circumstances. The Emperor Maximilian was on his deathbed in late 1518, and it was clear that he would not live for much longer. Pope Leo X wanted to curb Habsburg power in Europe by obstructing the succession of Maximilian's son, Charles to the Imperial throne. As a result Leo courted the favour of the Imperial Electors in the hope that an alternative Emperor might be elected. One of those electors was Frederick the Wise, Elector of Saxony. The Pope even sent Frederick a golden rose, the highest symbol of papal favour in the hope that this would sway his decision. It also meant that Leo was unlikely to antagonise Frederick by arresting Luther or acting harshly against him. Hence Luther won a hearing in the Imperial free city of Augsburg rather than Rome.

What was the significance of Luther's meeting with Eck in 1519?

In June 1519, Luther was involved in a set piece disputation (a debate) with **Johannes Eck**, a theologian

Johannes Eck (1486–1543) was Luther's main opponent. The turning point in his career as a theologian was the appearance of Luther, and other Protestant reformers. Apart from being an active proponent of Catholic ideas in debate, he wrote a number of works attacking Luther, Zwingli and other reformers. The most important of his works was *Arguments against Luther and Other Enemies of the Church*, first published in 1525.

from the University of Ingolstadt in Bavaria. The two met at Leipzig in order to debate the issue of papal primacy and the route to salvation. Luther was in the public spotlight against one of the finest minds in Europe. Eck is generally seen to have triumphed in this dispute because he successfully identified Luther with the fifteenth-century heretic Jan Hus. In fact, Luther himself admitted that he shared many of the views of the Bohemian reformer. Yet Luther maintained that if such views had the authority of scripture, then Hus was correct, just as he was. In short, how could such men be heretics if they were supported by the Word of God?

Luther was now putting himself into a very dangerous position. After all, Hus had been burned for his views. Over the course of 1518 and 1519 Luther had been forced into a radical position where he had denied some of the central features of Catholic doctrine. He had called into question issues such as papal primacy, purgatory, the status of priests and the role of good works. The Catholic authorities had failed to convince Luther of the error of his ways, and it was clear that Luther was moving further and further away from Roman Catholicism. In light of the Eck debate, 1520 would be a crucial year in the Lutheran Reformation as Luther laid out his doctrine on paper and faced the challenges of both Church and state.

Luther's increasing publicity was worrying for the papacy. Academic debates had not moved Luther; the time to increase the pressure had come. Eck journeyed to Rome soon after leaving Leipzig and helped draft the papal bull *Exsurge Domine*, which condemned 41 propositions drawn from Luther's work and threatened Luther with excommunication.

In June 1520, Leo X issued the bull *Exsurge Domine*, and both Eck and Girolamo Aleander were commissioned as special **nuncios** to publish the bull in the empire. *Exsurge Domine* opened with the phrase: 'Arise O Lord…a wild boar seeks to destroy the vineyard'. The boar was of course Luther and the papal bull gave Luther 60 days to **recant**, or face excommunication. Luther's response was to write, *Adversus Execrabilem Antichristi Bullam*, which proclaimed the Pope to be Antichrist and defiantly stated that: 'this thing shall neither console nor frighten me'. Most of northern and central Germany rejected the bull, and calls by Eck to burn the works of Luther were rejected in Cologne. On 3 January 1521, Luther was officially excommunicated by the bull *Decet Romanum Pontificem*. He could no longer attend communion and receive the Eucharist. He was now a rebel and an outcast. In typically defiant and almost showman style, **Luther burned the papal bull** and prepared to stand firm. More importantly, he started to lay down his teachings on paper.

THE THEOLOGY OF LUTHER

The year 1520 was an extremely busy one for Luther, as he had 24 works published. This was the year in which Luther explained his theology (views about God) in writing.

Luther's Three Great Works of 1520
1. *An Appeal to the Christian Nobility of the German Nation*, **August 1520**

What does *An Appeal to the Christian Nobility* tell us about Luther?

- The title itself reveals Luther's political conservatism. He is calling upon the princes to undertake and oversee reform. Luther believed that the princes had been given authority by God to rule, and it was their duty to usher in reform of the Church. Therefore whilst Luther was happy to court popular support he ultimately believed in Reformation from above, directed by political elites.
- Luther specifically mentions the *German Nation* in the title in a bid to tap into the nationalist sentiment that had developed around his cause. This pamphlet was written in German and directed towards the princes of Germany. Luther was very aware that many people viewed his struggle as a German one directed against the power of Rome.

What is *An Appeal to the Christian Nobility of the German Nation* about?

KEY EVENTS

Luther's **burning of the papal bull.** On 10 December 1520, a number of students and teachers from Wittenberg University were invited to the Elster gate in the town at 10 am. There they found Luther, who unceremoniously burned the bull and the works of his enemies, such as Eck, for good measure. He justified his actions by saying: 'Since they have burned my books, I burn theirs'. As with the pinning of the Ninety-Five Theses to the door of the Wittenberg Castle church, Luther deliberately made the burning of the bull a public event in order to popularise his stance.

KEY ISSUES

Luther's ideas as they are expressed in the three works of 1520 are important for **Key Issue 1** (see page iv).

*And though they [Popes] say that this authority was given to
St Peter when the keys were given to him, it is plain enough
that the keys were not given to St Peter alone, but to the whole
community.*

- Luther was deeply critical of papal power and abuses
  within the Church. Luther claimed that successive popes
  had failed to implement any meaningful reform despite
  the fact that abuses within the Church had been brought
  to their attention. Luther attacked the idea of papal
  infallibility in spiritual and doctrinal affairs.

*All Christians are truly of the spiritual estate, and there is no
difference amongst them, save of office alone.*

- Luther condemned the idea that priests were spiritually
  superior to ordinary men or that they were
  intermediaries between man and God. Luther
  highlighted the importance of man's personal
  relationship with God in a doctrine to be known as the
  priesthood of all believers. Ministers were to act as
  representatives of their congregations but were not
  superior, hence both laity and clergy would receive the
  bread and the wine at communion. This was known as
  communion in both kinds. As Luther himself wrote: 'we
  are all consecrated as priests by baptism'.

*It has been devised that the Pope, bishops, priests and monks
are called the spiritual estate; princes, lords, artificers and
peasants are the temporal estate. This is an artful lie and
hypocritical device…*

- The papacy had long argued that in extreme
  circumstances the Church could intervene in secular
  affairs but laymen could never get involved in spiritual
  matters. Luther asserted that the corruption of the
  Church was a secular matter and urged the princes to
  lead the way in overseeing reform. After all the papacy
  had failed to implement any positive changes. As Luther
  stated: 'the Pope almost seems to be the adversary of
  Christ called in Scripture the Antichrist'. Luther now
  called on the princes to take responsibility for spiritual
  matters in their territories.

2. *The Babylonish Captivity of the Church*, October 1520

What is the significance of the title?

- The title refers to the Old Testament story of the enslavement of the Jews by the Babylonians. Luther is trying to get people to see that true Christians were being enslaved by Rome in the same way that the Jews had been shackled by the Babylonians.
- Unlike *An Appeal to the Christian Nobility*, this work was written in Latin and was clearly aimed at an intellectual/educated audience. It was in the *Babylonish Captivity* that Luther outlined some key points of doctrine.

What can this work tell us about Luther's theology?

- By 1520 Luther's theological agenda was shaping up and it was clear that his ideas were very different to those of the Catholic Church. Works such as the *Babylonish Captivity* must have made it apparent to the Catholic authorities that there was little chance of any reconciliation with Luther.
- Luther claimed that four of the seven sacraments had no grounding in Scripture and therefore ceased to exist as holy sacraments. Luther identified only three sacraments: baptism, the Eucharist and penance. Only these three were uniquely Christian in that they had been established by Jesus and could be found in the New Testament. In time Luther would dispense with penance and settle for only two sacraments. This was a clear attack at the heart of Catholic doctrine and it did not go unnoticed. For moderates such as Erasmus, who up to now had been sympathetic to Luther's ideas, this was too much, and they began to distance themselves from the Lutheran movement. On reading the Babylonish Captivity, Erasmus exclaimed: 'the division is now beyond repair'.
- Luther's belief in the authority of Scripture was unmoving throughout his career. *Sola Scripitura* or scripture alone formed the basis of all Lutheran doctrine.
- In denying the sacrament of penance, Luther was re-affirming the idea that it was God who forgave sins

rather than priests. God was forgiving of error but this was a private matter between man and God. Luther now called into question the sanctity of the priesthood and the duty to dispense pardons.

- In denying the sacrament of ordination, Luther was attacking the status of the priesthood. Luther contested the idea that priests could make direct contact with God and as a result were superior to the ordinary laity. This ties in with Luther's doctrine on the priesthood of all believers and communion in both kinds. Luther himself writes: 'Of this sacrament the Church of Christ knows nothing: it was invented by the Church of the Pope'.

- Luther retained the Eucharist as a sacrament but challenged the idea of transubstantiation. Luther denied that a miracle took place during the Mass, and argued that the bread and the wine remained just that – bread and wine. For Luther, Christ had sacrificed himself once and for all, and this could not be recreated. The priest did not possess miracle-working powers. Yet Luther did not break entirely with Catholic tradition on the Eucharist. Later, more radical Protestant reformers such as **Zwingli** would view the Eucharist as a purely symbolic act. Luther still maintained that the real presence of Christ entered the Eucharist during Holy Communion. Luther explained the presence of Christ in the bread and wine as being like the presence of heat in hot iron. The iron remains iron but heat has entered it, just as the bread remains bread but Christ has entered it. Some of Luther's followers were surprised that Luther would make such concessions to Catholic theology.

3. *Of the Liberty of the Christian Man*, November 1520

What does the title reveal about Luther's theology?

- Luther's doctrine was a liberating one. It condemned ideas of spiritual hierarchy and superiority. Instead Luther encouraged a personal relationship between man and God. Luther highlighted the idea that no man could satisfactorily obey the laws of God, but that true believers would do their best to follow God's Word, and if they fell short then Christ would make up for it.

KEY PEOPLE

Huldrych Zwingli (1484–1531) was a Swiss reformer who entered the priesthood in Glarus. In 1526, he became convinced that doctrine and worship had to be guided by scripture, and his own beliefs became more evangelical in nature. In 1518, he took up the post of people's priest in Zurich where, over the next decade, he led a reform movement. In 1525, the Reformation in Zurich seemed complete with the abolition of the Mass. The views of Zwingli concerning *sola scriptura* and the Eucharist are laid out in his 67 articles of 1523. Most notably, Zwingli disagreed with Luther over the nature of the elements in the Eucharist, with Zwingli asserting that the bread and the wine remained just that during communion. Zwingli died in 1531 on the battlefield during the Second Kappel War. (See Chapter 5).

Justification by faith alone Luther argued that man was always a sinner in the eyes of God and could not secure salvation through good deeds on earth. Instead, man had to put his trust in God and seek salvation through true faith and the unselfish love that resulted. Good works may still be seen as a sign of salvation, but were now redundant as a cause of salvation.

Luther's doctrine of **justification by faith alone** or *sola fide* was therefore one of spiritual freedom.

- Luther even dedicated this work to Pope Leo X. Did Luther really believe that the Pope would support his ideas? Probably not, but given the radicalism of Luther's ideas to date it did no harm to be slightly more conciliatory towards Rome.

What was the significance of the Three Great Works?

- The gulf between Luther and Rome was wider than ever. Over the course of 1518 and 1519 Rome had tried to win Luther back to the Catholic fold, but as 1520 came to an end it became clear that Lutheran doctrine was irreconcilable with that of Catholicism.
- In October 1520 Luther received the Bull *Exsurge Domine* (see page 34) and it became clear that the Catholic authorities were ready to take a harder line on Luther. Luther had laid out his doctrine on paper and now he was going to have to stand by it before Pope and Emperor.

Luther's doctrinal position was now complete. Ideas which had been evolving over the course of 1517, 1518 and 1519 had now matured and were down on paper for all to see. The Great Works reflect Luther's confidence in his ideas and his readiness to attack central areas of Catholic belief.

Luther's audience

After 1520, Luther cleverly began to adapt his message to suit a wider audience. He knew that criticism of papal taxation would not fall on deaf ears in a Germany resentful of seeing their hard-earned money disappear over the Alps to a foreign figurehead they had never seen before. Moreover, communion in both kinds and the priesthood of all believers, if described simply, were messages of equality and freedom, which could appeal to peasants resentful of powerful landlords. Luther wrote countless pamphlets or *flugschriften*, which were eagerly received by the literate populace and read aloud to the rest. To say, therefore, that Luther's doctrine had little effect on the common man would be false, although just how much the laity actually understood is questionable. Many took from Luther's message what they wanted and ignored the rest.

THE EMPEROR INTERVENES

The Diet at Worms

In April 1521, Luther was summoned before His Imperial Majesty Charles V, **Holy Roman Emperor** and the most powerful man in Christendom. Indeed, Luther was fortunate to be given a hearing, as it would have been entirely appropriate for the emperor merely to endorse the bull of excommunication issued by Leo X. Luther could have been arrested without a further hearing and charged with heresy. Yet, due to the pressure placed upon him by the German princes, the young emperor decided to allow Luther a final chance to recant his views. Luther was even allowed to travel to and from Worms, where the **Imperial Diet** was to meet, under a promise of safe conduct. Jan Hus had travelled to the Council of Constance under such an agreement in 1415, yet he had not escaped the flames. Luther was in real danger and he knew it.

Luther's appearance at Worms displays the courage of the man, but he probably stood defiant safe in the knowledge that Charles V was unlikely to act rashly and provoke the wrath of the princes, or even popular unrest. One must remember that Charles had relied upon the votes of the Seven Electors of the Holy Roman Empire and to risk antagonising them after only two years of office would have been foolhardy. On 18 April 1521, Luther stood before Charles for the first and only time:

- Luther acknowledged his own writings and refused to recant, for to do so would not be right, as this very retraction would again bring about a state of affairs where: 'tyranny and impiety would rule and rage among the people of God'.
- Luther maintained his fundamental doctrines and the stand-off which had begun at Augsburg remained in place.

KEY ISSUES

The reaction of the Emperor to Luther and his ideas is important for **Key Issue 2** (see page iv).

KEY TERMS

The Holy Roman Empire was a sprawling mass of over 400 separate states in central Europe, including Germany. Nominally, the **Holy Roman Emperor**, from the time of Charlemagne, had ruled over these states but, in reality, there was little centralisation. Each state had its own laws, customs and privileges. The emperor himself was elected by princes from the seven most powerful principalities: Saxony, Palatinate, Brandenburg, the King of Bohemia, Mainz, Trier and Cologne. These princes were known as electors. Yet, by the time Charles V succeeded Maximilian in 1519, the position had become monopolised by the Austrian Habsburgs. Why? For princes keen to guard their rights and territories it was a case of better the devil you know. Besides which, the Habsburgs usually bribed the electors with large amounts of money!

KEY TERMS

The **Imperial Diet** was essentially the parliament of the Empire attended by princes and representatives of the imperial free cities. Imperial laws could be passed at the Diet.

The imperial response was a predictable one. Charles V denounced Luther as a heretic and ordered the bull *Decet Romanum* (1521) to be enacted immediately. The Edict of Worms stated that Luther's writings were to be burned and citizens of the empire were forbidden to house, feed or protect the heretic Luther. Both Church and emperor had now outlawed Luther, but Charles did stand by his word and allowed Luther to leave Worms unharmed.

The Holy Roman Empire.

What was the significance of the Diet of Worms in 1521?

Luther had been made a secular outlaw by Charles V. He had been condemned a heretic by the leading political figure in western Europe, and the papacy was ready to follow suit. Luther was in grave danger of becoming a martyr for his cause. Or was he? The historian Andrew Pettegree argues that the young Emperor was unlikely to act too rashly against Luther as he did not want to upset the princes and create civil unrest. Perhaps Luther was safer than he thought at Worms.

Indeed, it was going to be very difficult for the Emperor to enforce the Edict of Worms. The Empire itself was politically decentralised, and real political power lay with the princes. It was unlikely that princes who were sympathetic to Luther's cause would oversee the strict implementation of the Edict of Worms. The Emperor had no means of ensuring that the letter of the law was carried out.

Luther's resolve had been hardened by his interrogation at Worms. Once more it seems that the harder the authorities tried to push Luther, the more assured he became of his ideas. At Worms, Luther must have been concerned for his safety. Asked to recognise the legitimacy of his works, Luther asked for a day to mull things over before returning with the immortal words: 'my conscience is captive to the word of God, I cannot and I will not recant anything, for to go against conscience is neither right nor safe'. Luther's courageous defiance undoubtedly increased his popular support.

THE ROLE PLAYED BY FREDERICK THE WISE

The extent of Frederick's influence

An important factor in explaining the rise to prominence of Luther was the protection of his political lord, the Elector **Frederick of Saxony**. Frederick had supported Luther upon hearing of his stand against indulgences, not so much because he agreed with Luther's theological and moral stance but because he wanted to protect the academic reputation of the University of Wittenberg, as well as preserve his own territories from external influence and intervention – that is, intervention from Charles V.

The importance of Frederick was that he was one of the seven imperial electors and, as such, he held the right to vote on who would become emperor. Indeed, Charles had relied upon Frederick's vote in 1519, when he succeeded his grandfather Maximilian I. If Charles was to establish his authority in the Empire, then he would need the support of men such as Frederick.

KEY ISSUES

The reaction of the princes is important for **Key Issue 2** (see page iv).

KEY PEOPLE

Frederick III of Saxony (1463–1525) was Elector of Saxony from 1486 until his death, and sought to curb the power of Charles V over the state of Saxony. Frederick helped Luther by preventing the reformer's extradition to Rome in 1518, as well as protecting him and offering advice, most of which was relayed through his secretary, Spalatin. Not only had Charles relied upon Frederick in 1519 for his imperial vote, but he also owed him money, with debts dating back to 1497. It may have been for these reasons that Frederick was not sent the Edict of Worms and Charles did not take more forceful action. His nickname was Frederick the Wise.

Frederick the Wise, Elector of Saxony, by Cranach the Elder.

Therefore, the Elector of Saxony was a powerful ally for Luther. Just how powerful was demonstrated in the wake of the Edict of Worms. On his way back to Wittenberg after the Diet of 1521, Luther was kidnapped by men under the authority of Frederick and taken for his own safety to Wartburg Castle. The young Charles V made no attempt to seek him out or have him arrested. The potential power of the princes in the Empire had been clearly demonstrated. Luther spent his time at Wartburg translating the New Testament into German, thereby opening up the scriptures to the people. While he was safe, the movement grew around him, and it became clear that Luther would have to return to Wittenberg to oversee its development.

CONCLUSION

In many ways the Diet of Worms represents a watershed mark in the career of Martin Luther. The secular condemnation by the emperor and princes at the Diet of Worms of 1521, following the clerical denouncement by the Pope the previous year, put Luther in a new light. No longer was this an individual pursuing a theological debate. Luther was now a condemned heretic around whom a popular movement was developing. Indeed, there are signs even before Worms that Luther was becoming a popular figure throughout Germany. In February, the papal **legate**, Aleander, reported that the whole of Germany was in revolt and that: 'nine out of ten people cry Luther and the rest death to the Roman **Curia**'. Moreover, Aleander promptly ordered a burning of Luther's books in Cologne. Yet he was one of the few to actively carry out the Edict of Worms.

There is little doubt that, by 1521, the message of Luther had found receptive ground in his homeland.

KEY TERMS

Legate A legate was a papal ambassador whose job it was to relate the views and policies of the Pope to foreign courts.

The **Curia** was the papal civil service or administrative unit.

ACTIVITY

1. Use your own knowledge to work out the context of Source 1. What was happening in 1518 when this source was written? How does this explain the purpose of Leo in writing this letter?

2. Think carefully about the author and the recipient of the letter in Source 1. What do we know of them? How does this explain the tone of the letter?

Source 1: The pope appeals to the ruler of Electoral Saxony not to protect Luther, one of the German prince's own subjects.

A certain son of wickedness, Martin Luther, as though relying on your protection, fears the authority or rebuke of no one. Although we know this is false, yet we write to your Lordship, urging that you retain the splendour of your glory and race unsoiled by such accusations. We appeal to your Lordship, for the sake of God's honour and ours and your own, please to give help that this Martin Luther may be delivered into the power and judgment of Rome.

3. What is Luther saying about the authority of the
   Bible in Source 2?

Source 2

*If we quote the Bible to the Church authorities, they object
that only the Pope can interpret it. It is a wicked fable that
only the Pope can interpret the Bible. The Church authorities
have seized this authority for themselves. Spiritual authority
was not given only to the Pope but to the whole community. If
we believe in the priesthood of all believers, should we not
have the power to examine and decide what is right or wrong
in religious matters? The Bible should make us free and bold,
and the spirit of freedom should not be chased away by the
inventions of the Pope.*

Martin Luther, *An Appeal to the
Christian Nobility of the German Nation*, 1520

4. Are you surprised by the tone that Luther adopts in
   the letter in Source 3? Explain your answer using
   your own knowledge. Think about why Luther might
   have written this letter to Frederick in 1522.

Source 3: Luther explains his attitude to obeying the
wishes of his own prince.

*I have done sufficient for your Grace this year by remaining in
my forced seclusion.*

*I come to Wittenberg under higher protection than that of the
Elector, and I have not the slightest intention of asking for
your Electoral Highness' help. For I consider that I am more
able to protect your Grace than you are to protect me. In this
matter God alone must manage without any human
intervention. Therefore he whose faith is greatest will receive
the most protection.*

Martin Luther, letter to the
Elector Frederick of Saxony, 1522

Enquiries
Study Sources A and B

> Compare these Sources as evidence for attitudes to indulgences.

Source A: From the Bull, *Salvator Noster* of Pope Sixtus IV.

Our aim is that the salvation of souls may be secured above all at that time when they most need the intercessions of others and are least able to help themselves. We wish by our Apostolic authority to draw on the treasury of the Church and to succour the souls in purgatory who died united with Christ through love and whose lives have merited that such intercessions should now be offered through an Indulgence of this kind.

With the longings of such great paternal affection as with God's help we can achieve, in reliance on the divine mercy and fullness of our power. It is our will that full remission should follow for the said souls in purgatory, to win them relief from their punishments.

Salvator Noster, August 1476

Source B: Martin Luther commenting on Indulgences.

Even if indulgences are the very merit of Christ and his saints and are therefore to be received with all reverence, in practice they have become the most disgraceful agency of greed. For is anyone using them to seek the salvation of men's souls, rather than the cash out of their purses? This is plain and obvious from their own ministry: for the ministers never preach anything else but to commend indulgences and to arouse the people to contribute. You will not hear from them who is to teach people, or what indulgences are, or on what day they apply and cease to apply, but only how much they ought to contribute.

The Pope is cruel if he does not grant to souls for nothing what he is able to grant the Church for the necessary fee.

Martin Luther, 1516

CHAPTER 3

What were the reasons for the success of Lutheranism?

EARLY SETBACKS

Andreas Karlstadt

Amid the remarkable success of Lutheranism during the period 1521–5, there were also some serious moments of crisis. When Luther returned to Wittenberg in 1522 after his period of captivity in Wartburg Castle he faced a local populace influenced by Andreas Karlstadt, a colleague of Luther at the University of Wittenberg. In Luther's absence, <u>Karlstadt had assumed the lead role in Church government at the expense of Philip Melanchthon</u>. Luther was concerned that Karlstadt was proposing more radical and quicker change than he had envisaged:

- Among Karlstadt's ideas was the need to cleanse churches immediately of images and altars, using violence if necessary. Karlstadt encouraged the smashing of statues of saints, images of God and religious pictures in churches, a process known as iconoclasm. Protestants believed that churches should be simple and basic places of worship. Statues and ornamentation were seen as idolatrous and an obstruction to man's relationship with God.
- Already, Karlstadt had taken a fifteen-year-old wife, named Anna von Mochau. Protestant reformers could find no scriptural text which forbade clergy from marrying and Karlstadt encouraged monks and priests to find themselves a wife.
- Moreover, Karlstadt and his followers welcomed the extremist group named the **Zwickau Prophets** into the town, and it was becoming clear that the word of God was being used as a vehicle for radical change and that order was in danger of being lost.
- Karlstadt differed from Luther over the central moment in the Mass. Whereas Luther argued that the bread and wine should still be offered up as a mark of reverence,

KEY TERMS

The **Zwickau Prophets** were a group from nearby Bohemia. Among their claims were the suggestions that they were in close communication with God, had no need of the Bible and that the ungodly should be slaughtered!

Karlstadt disagreed, believing that there should be no sign of sacrifice.

Between 1521 and 1522, Wittenberg became a hotbed of religious change. It was not unknown for priests and monks to marry nuns from the local convent! Some priests conducted religious services in their own clothes. Notably, the friar Gabriel Zwilling celebrated the Lord's Supper wearing a beret with a feather in it! Luther returned to Wittenberg in March 1522. He put on his Augustinian robes and deliverd eight sermons on eight successive days. These were known at his Invocavit sermons, in which Luther denounced Karlstadt's reforms and his use of force in implementing them. Luther had demonstrated his conservatism for all to see. In doing so he had taken back control of the Reformation and highlighted the importance of the spoken word in the process.

THE PEASANTS' REVOLT, 1525

Background to the revolt

The Lutheran message undoubtedly made an impact in the countryside among the peasant population. Luther's message was initially a flexible one and an accessible one, as woodcuts and rhyming passages, along with Lutheran missionaries from the cities, opened up the scriptures to the rural community. While at Worms in 1521, Luther had awoken one morning to find the sign of revolutionary peasants, the *Bundschuh* (clog), painted on doors throughout the town in support of his stance. Yet there was a danger that Luther's message might be misinterpreted, or reinterpreted, if too much flexibility and freedom was allowed.

Although the peasants essentially owed allegiance to their lord and paid dues and taxes to him, rural communities were run by village communes. These communes had significant powers in overseeing local affairs and the reforms proposed by Luther gave them an opportunity to take greater control over the Church and challenge the existing feudal order. Rising prices and pressure on land, combined with discontent over taxation, provided social and economic stimulus for reform.

KEY ISSUES

The effects of Lutheranism on the peasants is important for **Key Issue 3** (see page iv).

Rebellious peasants.

Despite Luther's attack on superstition, peasant society was deeply conservative. In astrological predictions, the year 1524 had been identified as a year of rebellion; in 1523 there were no less than 51 tracts speculating on the subject. This prophecy increased tension in the countryside considerably.

Throughout Germany, attempts to arrest Lutheran ministers, as part of the enforcement of the Edict of Worms, often led to a peasant reaction in defence of Lutheranism. It is not hard to see how Luther's message of the priesthood of all believers and the attack on clerical hierarchy could be adapted to mirror the landlord/peasant relationship. Essentially, the idea of spiritual equality was equated with secular equality. German peasants were little more than serfs, tied to the land with little opportunity to move from one estate to another. As the population rose, land was in increasingly short supply, and landlords exploited the shortage to gain cheap labour. Increased taxation and a series of poor harvests exacerbaed the situation and served to make Luther's message all the more appealing to the peasantry.

The Twelve Articles

Following disorder in the Black Forest area in June 1524, the Peasants' War began in earnest in March 1525 when the peasants of southern Germany rebelled against the ruling classes. The uprisings were localised and varied in intensity and scale from region to region. The revolt spread rapidly throughout the south from its original breeding grounds of Baden and Sawbia; Bavaria, however, witnessed little unrest. This was partly down to the Duke having kept the land-owning nobility in check over the previous decade, ensuring a more just lot for the peasantry. Bavaria was an exception, however, as between March and May 1525 the revolt spread to the centre and to parts of the north of the Empire. Peasant armies targeted noble estates and Church property, bringing more than an element of class warfare to the struggle. In Salzburg and the Tyrol monasteries were looted and nobles murdered.

That said, the Peasants' Revolt was not just concerned with mindless violence. In March 1525 a manifesto for change emerged, and would serve as a model for most of the peasants in revolt. The manifesto was called *The Twelve Articles of Memmingen*, and gives us a clear insight into the grievances of the peasants in 1525, demonstrating equally how socio-economic concerns were merged with religious ones. The *Twelve Articles* outlined the following key points:

- Communities should have the right to elect their own ministers – this was very much a feature of the infant Lutheran Church.
- Serfdom was denounced as unjust and landlords were vehemently criticised for their exploitation of the peasantry. The influence of Luther was reflected in the assertion that Christ died for everyone and that peasants were not the property of their landlords. The message of equality and justice based on godly law shines through in the *Twelve Articles*. It was this message and the violence that accompanied it that shook the ruling classes to the core in 1525.

- Peasant rights were to be restored in the countryside. Peasants were to have access to forests, communal grazing land and waterways. All of these areas had steadily been regulated by the landowners, particularly in the south west of Germany.
- Economic grievances were also expressed in relation to unmanageable levels of rent and unreasonable labour services.

The Significance of the *Twelve Articles*

Grievances such as those outlined in the *Twelve Articles* were not new, and their resonance varied from region to region. It could be argued that such peasant manifestos represented only the views of the better off peasant classes, and that ordinary commoners sought only mindless blood-letting and pillage. Yet the *Twelve Articles* were a crucial document, demonstrating that the Reformation message had reached the countryside and was used to frame grievances. Peasant discontent was legitimised by an appeal to divine law and given extra impetus by Luther. Without Luther there would have been no revolt in 1525: the peasants were galvanised by the Word of God.

The Tyrolean Constitution

As the uprising spread north the Peasants' Revolt ceased to be a purely rural phenomenon. Cities and towns in Thuringia and Franconia witnessed unrest, whilst in the east the miners of the Tyrol joined with the peasants. Here a rebel leader named Michael Gaismair drafted the Tyrolean Constitution, in which he set out his radical vision of a Christian republic. In the sixteenth century it was taken for granted that monarchs and princes ruled over states in accordance with God's wishes. There was a strict hierarchy set in place by God, and to challenge that structure was to commit an act of sedition and rebellion. Gaismair's alternative form of government, in which social privileges and the class system were to disappear, was therefore an extremely radical proposition. The idea of a democratic republic with a self-sufficient economy was somewhat ahead of its time, and, like other rebel agendas, was never going to go beyond the paper it was printed on. The Tyrolean Constitution demonstrates, however, that some peasant leaders were politically astute, and that the revolt was about more than just mindless destruction.

Thomas Müntzer

In Thuringia, on the borders of Saxony, a man named Thomas Müntzer led peasant troops into battle. Müntzer was a radical pastor who had a different vision of the Reformation from Luther – Müntzer wanted to prepare the world for the Second Coming of Christ, and to that end he urged his followers to slaughter the Godless lords. Müntzer believed that he and his followers were part of the elect, chosen by God for salvation. It was therefore their duty to follow him in God's task, eliminating the Godless. Müntzer's apocalyptic vision that the end of the world was close at hand made the duty of heralding the empire of Christ more urgent and convinced him of the certainty of victory. Unsurprisingly, the combined forces of the Lutheran Philip of Hesse and the staunchly Catholic Duke George of Saxony defeated Müntzer's band of peasants at the Battle of Frankenhausen in May 1525.

What was the significance of the Peasants' Revolt?

By the end of the Peasant's Revolt nearly 100,000 people had lost their lives, 270 castles and 52 cloisters had been destroyed and the course of the Reformation had changed in Germany.

- In some regions it is clear that the peasants had an idea of the political and social changes they wished to bring about and in others, where leadership was less in evidence, the uprisings generated little more than destruction.
- The peasant armies were defeated with relative ease by the Swabian League, a regional defence force made up of troops supplied by princes and cities. Little mercy was shown to rebel leaders, such as Müntzer, who were executed.
- It could be argued that, in the wake of the uprising, some landowners were more sympathetic to the cause of the common man and more respectful of peasants' rights. In this sense the revolt can be seen as achieving its initial aim of alleviating the strain of oppression that the peasants were under, although in many areas the exploitation of the peasants continued.
- Luther had initially shown some sympathy to the plight of the peasants, but he did not condone violence. Clearly

In his **Admonition to Peace**, Luther reproaches the peasants for using violence and particularly objects to their use of the Gospel to justify it. It also criticises the princes:

'we have no one on earth to thank for this disastrous rebellion except you princes and lords ... as temporal rulers you do nothing but cheat and rob the people so that you may lead a life of luxury and extravagance. The poor common people cannot bear it any longer...'

he recognised that his message of equality and freedom had made a profound impact in the south of Germany, but he was unprepared for the scale of the unrest. In April 1525 Luther wrote his *Admonition to Peace* in a bid to subdue the rebels. One month later he condemned the revolt in his work *Against the Thieving, Murdering Hordes of Peasants*. Here he called on the princes to crush the rebellion and show no mercy to the peasants. It would appear that the popular Reformation was over.

- As a direct result of the events of 1525 both Luther and the princes became aware of the explosive nature of the Reformation message. Consequently, the Reformation increasingly came under princely control as the ruling classes sought to harness Luther's appeal and ideas. The Word of God could not make people free and bold if it also undermined the social hierarchy.

Significance of these early setbacks

The actions of Andreas Karlstadt and the Peasants' Revolt were significant for three reasons:

- They confirmed Luther's belief that reform had to be initiated and guided from above; that is, from the city magistrates and princes as outlined in his treatise *Address to the Christian Nobility of the German Nation* (1520).
- These events also emphasised for Luther the dangers of allowing the laity to read the scriptures and interpret the word of God for themselves. Preachers and teachers were deemed necessary in order to guide and instruct.
- Karlstadt and the peasants demonstrated that Lutheranism could not be the all-embracing movement it had threatened to become during the period 1520–5. The peasants were largely alienated by the events of 1525. As it became clear that Lutheranism was developing as a conservative movement under the guidance of the princes, extremist splinter groups emerged such as the Anabaptists (see page 100).

By 1525, Lutheranism had developed into a popular movement. What had begun merely as a theological, academic debate had exploded into a powerful protest which found support in the cities and the countryside. The implications of this movement were profound as, by 1555,

Germany would have two faiths recognised by the Religious Peace of Augsburg. In short, the whole structure and order of religious life in Germany would change as a result of the success of Lutheranism. In order to explain the success of Luther's challenge one must look not only at the role of the individual himself, but also at the environment in which he operated. Crucial to the success of the movement were the following factors:

- The nature and accessibility of Luther's message was of central importance to the success of the movement.
- Luther was a brave and courageous man.
- Circumstances unquestionably favoured Luther, as he was able to exploit widespread German anticlericalism and appeal to patriotic sentiment.
- The protection that Luther received from some princes such as Frederick the Wise and later, and more importantly, Philip of Hesse (see page 81), allowed the movement to develop in the face of a troubled and inexperienced Holy Roman Emperor.
- Princely support became more organised and official in the form of leagues established in 1526 at Torgau and in 1531 at Schmalkalden to defend Lutheranism.

Therefore, Lutheranism saw two phases during the period leading up to 1555.

- From 1520 to 1529, Lutheranism emerged quickly and spectacularly as a mass movement.
- From 1530 to 1555, the movement became increasingly shaped by the actions of the princes and one could argue that, in their hands, Lutheranism was consolidated and politicised.

HOW DID LUTHERANISM BECOME A POPULAR MOVEMENT BY 1525?

The role of individuals
Martin Luther
Clearly one cannot discuss the success of Lutheranism without assessing the importance of its founder, Martin

Luther. As we have already seen, Luther initiated the challenge to the existing Catholic Church through his condemnation of its practices and doctrine. Moreover, Luther displayed great courage in maintaining his position and standing firm in the face of the accusations and threats made by Cardinal Cajetan, John Eck, the papacy and the Holy Roman Emperor, Charles V. Furthermore, Luther's energy and creativity resulted in a mass of literature, and it would be fair to say that, by 1521, Luther had laid down his theological agenda on paper. His agenda was epitomised by the three great works of 1520 (see page 35).

(see page 35)

There were other individuals who undertook the task of spreading ideas of reform. In north Germany, **Johannes Bugenhagen** carried out much work in organising reform. Yet Luther was not just one reformer among many; he was exceptional. It was Luther who drove the Reformation in the early years, writing and printing with unbelievable vigour. It was Luther to whom the people looked as a figurehead and talisman. While his influence may have diminished after 1530, Luther remained a crucial figure, for it was he who maintained the authority of pure gospel amid Catholic threats, and it was he who was increasingly seen as a German hero by the common man. Luther very skilfully tapped into the anticlericalism that existed in Germany and deliberately adapted the Lutheran message to fit varying audiences and circumstances.

Philip Melanchthon

It is important to also consider the role of Luther's young protégé, Philip Melanchthon. It was he who wrote the first systematic and pure work of the new faith in 1521, entitled *Loci Communes*. Bearing in mind that Luther was effectively in captivity in Wartburg Castle between 1521 and 1522, other scholarly individuals were required to make an impact. Melanchthon was the most important, not only in laying out an organised explanation of the new faith, but also in trying to restrict the radical tendencies of others, such as Andreas Karlstadt, who wanted to accelerate the rate of reform and change. Notably, it was Melanchthon who, in 1530, drew up the Confession of Augsburg – the Lutheran statement of belief.

The flexibility of Luther's messages

Furthermore, the publication of a **German New Testament** in 1522 was a major contribution to the early Reformation in Germany. This was because the scriptures were now in the mother tongue and therefore accessible to the literate section of the population. The message of justification by faith alone and the primacy of the scriptures had been set out by Luther and, by 1521, this message was gradually spreading from the cities into the countryside, through the mediums of **printing** and **preaching**. Perhaps most importantly during these early years of success (1521–5), the movement was broad ranging, in both its appeal and its support. It must be stressed that this was a deliberate ploy by Luther. The Lutheran message was a flexible one and Luther readily adapted it to suit differing audiences. In some ways the people of Germany took from Luther's message what they wanted.

The so-called nurseries of the Reformation were the cities, such as Nuremberg, where a disproportionately literate population could be found. This was a population more likely to understand the finer points of Luther's theology,

KEY ISSUES

The appeal of Luther's ideas to people is important for **Key Issue 1** (see page iv).

KEY TERM

German New Testament. Luther translated the New Testament from Greek (probably using the edition produced by Erasmus) into German between January and March 1522 while in Wartburg, although he continued to tinker with the translation until his death. With the mother tongue being increasingly used for church services across Germany, the need for such a translation was great and the final result has been viewed as one of the most important contributions to German literature.

Printing Fortunately for Luther he was able to make use of a relatively new invention, in the form of the printing press (see page 60). The first press was put into production by Gutenberg in 1455 and by 1500 there were printing shops in over 60 German cities. The mass production of cheap pamphlets was crucial to the spread of Lutheranism.

Preaching The purpose of Luther's sermons was to instruct the people in the new doctrine and to encourage them to support and follow the movement. Luther had thousands of his sermons published in order that travelling preachers could read his words aloud to the people. The most notable of Luther's sermons were the series of Christmas and Advent sermons published in 1522.

and identify with it. Therefore, while the artisan in Augsburg might not understand the intricacies of the priesthood of all believers, he would identify with the anticlerical message that went alongside it.

Yet perhaps as much as 90 per cent of the German population lived and worked in the countryside and, if the movement was to become truly popular, it would have to spread from its original home in the cities. The fact that it did, especially in the south, was partly due to the flexibility of the message. Moreover, in the countryside, local village leaders saw the Reformation as a chance to establish greater control over the parish church at the expense of the existing clergy. Yet there was obviously a danger in allowing such flexibility, in that Luther's message could be misread and adopted for more radical purposes, something Luther did not want. As we have seen, this is what happened in 1525 with the Peasants' Revolt.

The printing press

The printing press was crucial to the dissemination of Luther's message for a number of reasons:

- The exact replication of multiple copies made doctrinal inaccuracies a thing of the past. Luther could attack mistranslations of Latin Bibles and commentaries from a position of real strength.
- Increasingly Luther wrote in the vernacular, in German. This served to open up his ideas to a wider audience and increase his popular, patriotic appeal. In 1526 his *German Mass* appeared, to be followed by his *Small Catechism* in 1529.
- Luther's doctrine rested on Scripture. His belief in *sola scriptura* was reinforced by the printing press which opened up the word of God to the people. In 1522 Luther translated the New Testament into German and within twelve years 200,000 copies had been sold. Bibles were expensive but one did not have to possess a Bible to hear the word of God being spoken. As Luther himself commented: 'ears are the most important organ of a true Christian'.
- Vernacular catechisms were also published by which the people gained instruction in what and how to worship.

Luther stated that: 'the catechism is the layman's Bible, it contains the whole of what every Christian must know of Christian doctrine'.

- Luther's ideas could spread quickly. Within weeks of posting the Ninety-Five Theses on the Castle Church door in Wittenberg, Luther's controversial views on indulgences had reached Magdeburg, Leipzig and Nuremberg.
- Pamphlets or *flugshriften* were quick and relatively cheap to produce. There were at least 6,000 separate publications in the German speaking lands during the 1520s alone.

To Luther the printed word was: 'God's highest and extremist act of grace, whereby the business of the Gospel is driven forward'. Luther was energetic in his publication of works. As towns grew in size and printing presses became more common, so the book trade grew. Literacy rates increased in cities and by the mid 1520s Luther and his supporters had begun to dominate the book market. In 1523 one third of the 498 titles published were written personally by Luther. The printing press allowed these works to reach a widespread audience. The printed word therefore revolutionised the Reformation message and facilitated its dissemination on a number of levels.

What were the other means by which Luther's message could be spread?

The printed word was only one means of persuading people to support Luther.

- The visual image played a crucial part in the success and appeal of the Reformation message. Luther and his supporters used **woodcuts** as a means of bridging the gap between the masses and the intellectuals. Images were clear, simple and often crude condemnations of the papacy and the Catholic Church.
- Music also played a prominent role for Luther in winning over the German people to his ideas. The singing of psalms and hymns became a fundamental part of Lutheran worship and Luther himself wrote over twenty Wittenberg hymns which were of course printed and disseminated across Germany. The historian Veit

A woodcut of Luther preaching.

argues that in some ways music broke down social barriers and therefore acted as a sign of solidarity amongst Protestants.

- Religious plays were used to facilitate the teaching of the Reformation message and to poke fun at the Catholic Church. Drama contained all forms of communication in one: singing, dancing and the visual aspects combining to make it an important means of conversion and instruction.

The situation in the Holy Roman Empire

One really ought not to talk of Germany during this period, but rather a Holy Roman Empire made up of over 400 small and politically autonomous states. Yet there is little doubt that the circumstances that existed in the Empire meant that Luther's message was guaranteed to find fertile ground among the people of the German states.

- The anticlericalism that existed in Germany has already been discussed (see page 17), but it needs to be stressed that opposition to Rome and discontent with the Catholic Church gave Luther the opportunity to set out his programme of reform and espouse the pure gospel.

- Moreover, the people of Germany were ready to identify with one of their own. Luther became a figure of German nationalism, a patriotic icon around whom the people could put forward their grievances with the Church. Events such as the disputation with Eck in 1519 or the Diet of Worms in 1521 merely enhanced Luther's image as an honest, courageous and worthy German battling against the odds to overcome the powerful and corrupt forces of the papacy.
- The common man could identify more with Luther than with a foreign figurehead residing hundreds of miles away. Luther rode on the back of such patriotic sentiment, writing specifically to the nobility of the German nation in 1520 (see page 35).
- Furthermore, the publication of a New Testament in German in 1522 had an enormous impact, selling out within three months and going through another 300 editions before Luther's death in 1546. Not only does this illustrate his popularity but also the readiness of the people to read the scriptures in their own language. Moreover, the Emperor's fear of executing such a popular national figure perhaps ensured Luther's survival in 1521 at Worms.

The German states

The German states were also well suited to receiving Luther's message:

KEY ISSUES

The effect of Luther's ideas on towns and cities is important for **Key Issue 3** (see page iv).

- The Holy Roman Empire contained a relatively large number of cities. Whereas England had only one city of any size, namely London (with a population of around 100,000), the Holy Roman Empire had several. Nuremberg, Augsburg and Hamburg all housed between 50,000 and 100,000 people, while Bremen, Lübeck and Magdeburg had between 20,000 and 50,000 inhabitants during the sixteenth century.
- These cities not only provided a large and disproportionately literate population, among whom the message could be spread, but they also contained universities and printing presses where the word of God could be translated and printed. Lutheran preachers spread the word among the majority who were illiterate. Woodcuts, images and illustrations were also produced

to accompany the written word and to disseminate the message among as many as possible (see page 58).

- One should also not forget that cities such as Hamburg lay on internal and external trade routes, which allowed the message to spread widely among the merchant classes.

It was in the cities that the German Reformation took off between 1521 and 1525, with the people providing the pressure on the local authority to embrace reform.

Charles V (1500–58)

Charles V is perhaps the most important political figure in sixteenth-century Europe. His inheritance was massive. On the death of his father, Philip I, he took over the Netherlands, Luxemburg and Franche-Comté while, on the death of his grandfather Ferdinand of Aragon, he became King of Castile and Aragon and ruler of Navarre, Sicily and Naples. The death of his other grandfather, Maximilian, in 1519, opened the door to Austrian Habsburg lands and the Holy Roman Empire.

Charles was only nineteen when he was elected emperor in 1519. He was inexperienced and needed the support of the princes, a dependence that ensured Luther's survival at Worms in 1521. Had Charles been able to remain in the Empire and devote more energy to the task of unifying the Church, he might well, with time, have succeeded. Yet the longer he was absent, the stronger and more accepted Lutheranism became. The vast nature of Charles V's inheritance and Empire meant that he was unable to give his full attention to the spread of Lutheranism in Germany. Indeed, during that crucial period of 1522–9, Charles was not present in Germany. The Emperor's preoccupation with the French threat in northern Italy and rebellions in Castile and Valencia in Spain allowed Lutheranism to gain a foothold so that, when in 1543 Charles entered Germany for only the third time, he was confronted with an irresolvable problem.

Charles delegated responsibility for the day-to-day running of the Empire to his brother, Ferdinand, yet too often the imperial policy was one of playing for time in order to

allow Charles to direct his attentions and finances elsewhere. For example, in 1526 at the Diet of Speyer (see page 72), the decision was made to allow princes to decide upon the implementation of the Edict of Worms. The result was that those in favour of reform, such as Hesse, did not enforce it. Charles would have liked to have been more decisive, yet this was not possible because of the threat of the **Ottoman Empire** in the Mediterranean and the continuing battle with the French king, Francis I, over Italy.

Protection and support
The nobility
We have already seen the role of Frederick the Wise in supporting and protecting Luther during and after the Diet of Worms, although one would hardly call him a

Ottoman Empire The most successful and powerful state in Europe between 1450 and 1600. Its navy controlled the Mediterranean, its army was formidable. The leader of the Empire between 1520 and 1566 was Suleiman the Magnificent. In 1529, he laid siege to the Habsburg capital Vienna, and in 1540 large parts of Hungary were annexed, thus proving that the Ottoman Empire was a constant threat to Charles.

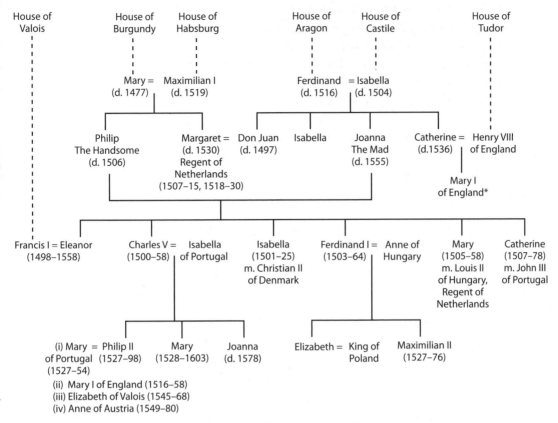

The Habsburg family tree, showing links to royal houses.

Family tree text (as labelled in the diagram):

House of Valois

House of Burgundy

House of Habsburg

House of Aragon

House of Castile

House of Tudor

Mary (d. 1477) = Maximilian I (d. 1519)

Ferdinand (d. 1516) = Isabella (d. 1504)

Philip The Handsome (d. 1506)

Margaret (d. 1530) Regent of Netherlands (1507–15, 1518–30) = Don Juan (d. 1497)

Isabella

Joanna The Mad (d. 1555)

Catherine (d.1536) = Henry VIII of England

Mary I of England*

Francis I = Eleanor (1498–1558)

Charles V (1500–58) = Isabella of Portugal

Isabella (1501–25) m. Christian II of Denmark

Ferdinand I (1503–64) = Anne of Hungary

Mary (1505–58) m. Louis II of Hungary, Regent of Netherlands

Catherine (1507–78) m. John III of Portugal

(i) Mary = Philip II of Portugal (1527–98) (1527–54)
(ii) Mary I of England (1516–58)
(iii) Elizabeth of Valois (1545–68)
(iv) Anne of Austria (1549–80)

Mary (1528–1603)

Joanna (d. 1578)

Elizabeth = King of Poland

Maximilian II (1527–76)

KEY ISSUES

The effects of Lutheranism on German princes and knights are important for **Key Issue 3** (see page iv).

KEY TERMS

Pacifist A pacifist is someone who believes in peace and is therefore opposed to violence or use of arms as a means of settling disputes.

committed Lutheran. Few other princes leapt to Luther's defence during the early years of the Reformation, primarily because they did not initially want to identify themselves with such a radical movement. The success of Lutheranism was by no means guaranteed and, while Luther specifically appealed to the German nobility in 1520 for support in reforming the Church, they remained aloof, preferring to see how Lutheranism would develop. In some senses, it was just too risky for the princes to back Luther during the early years.

The Imperial Knights

Luther himself was wary of armed support, as he maintained a strictly **pacifist** approach to reform at this stage. Luther's position was illustrated in 1521 when he refused the support of the Imperial Knights, an independent group of minor noblemen whose forefathers had been extremely influential during the Middle Ages, but whose influence had now waned. They did, however, possess military backing and were ready to raise arms in Luther's name against the Emperor and some German princes. In particular, one of their humanist leaders, Ulrich von Hutten, recognised the national appeal of Luther. Luther declined their assistance on two counts:

- He already had the influential support of Frederick the Wise.
- There was little to be gained by such violent methods at this stage.

Luther was proved correct in his judgement when, in 1523, another of the knights' leaders, Franz von Sickingen, was defeated by a group of local princes after he had attempted to seize the Archbishopric of Trier.

As Lutheranism became a stronger and accepted force from the mid-1520s onwards, some princes gradually changed their views and moved to support Luther. The first to do so was Albrecht of Hohenzollern, Grand Master of the Teutonic Knights, followed in 1526 by Philip of Hesse. Indeed, in 1526, a group of Lutheran princes emerged in the form of the League of Torgau, led by the Elector of Saxony and Hesse and designed to prevent the implementation of the Edict of Worms. When the princes became Lutheran, they turned their subjects over to the new faith, either because they themselves were committed believers in Luther's message or because of public pressure in favour of Luther. The material benefits of secularising Church lands also appealed to the German princes. Generally, the role of the princes was far more important after 1530, when the movement was largely in their hands and became more conservative in nature as a result.

WHAT DID IT MEAN FOR A TOWN TO BECOME LUTHERAN?

The towns and cities, as we have seen, were areas of spectacular success for Lutheranism, illustrated by the fact that, by 1550, a total of 50 out of the 65 imperial cities were adhering to the new faith. The decision to adopt

Lutheranism generally came from the town council, yet often it was under severe pressure from the local populace to do so. By 1525, Erfurt, Magdeburg, Nuremberg and Bremen had embraced reform. Augsburg and Strasburg joined them in 1534. However, to abandon Catholicism was one thing but to set up a new church structure was quite another and often proved problematic. Generally, adopting Lutheranism meant a number of changes:

The Catholic Mass was abolished and replaced by a German Mass or communion rite. The *Deutsche Messe* written by Luther was published in 1526 and acted as the new, reformed liturgy.

- Communion in both kinds was introduced.
- Altars and images were removed from churches.
- Baptismal and marital services were performed in German.
- Clerical marriage was permitted.
- A reformed catechism was introduced, through which the laity could be educated in the new faith. Luther published two catechisms in German in 1529.
- The clergy were re-educated in the new faith. Initially, itinerant (travelling from place to place) Lutheran preachers had a large role to play in the preaching of the gospel. Men such as Andreas Osiander in Nuremberg were very important.
- The territorial prince was responsible for the uniform practice of religion. The ruler of each state would appoint visitors whose job it was to investigate worship in the parishes of the state and ensure that good practice was being observed.

The adoption of a new Church structure was always going to be a lengthy and difficult process. Luther soon became aware, through the radicalism of Karlstadt in 1522 and the Peasants' Revolt of 1525, that the scriptures could not be left entirely in the hands of the people, and city magistrates and princes were urged to guide reform. It was up to men such as Melanchthon and Bugenhagen to establish a Church structure that incorporated a trained ministry.

The reaction of Erasmus and the Christian humanists

After 1525, the movement became more political and consolidation was in the hands of the princes. However, while describing the movement as conservative, one must not forget just how radical and revolutionary the initial challenge had been. Indeed, it was too radical for the great humanist Desiderius Erasmus. In 1524, he wrote against Luther for the first time in his work. *On the Freedom of the Will* specifically denounced Luther's doctrine of justification by faith alone. The ageing Erasmus had stayed loyal to his Catholic roots, which was not surprising given the status and wealth he had accumulated over the years. He had too much to lose by supporting Luther. The humanistic criticism and scriptural enquiry of Erasmus had once inspired Luther, and their split in 1525, sealed with Luther's retaliatory *On the Bondage of the Will*, was symbolic of how far Lutheranism had come. Younger humanists with less to lose tended to remain with Luther.

ACTIVITY

1. Where is Luther when he writes the letter in Source 1?
2. What was his purpose in writing the letter in Source 1?
3. How is the utility of the source affected by the fact that Luther is writing to Melanchthon?

Source 1

I do not approve of your moderation towards these radicals. We should not immediately accept their views but test them out from the Bible. You should enquire about their spiritual condition. Do not approve of them simply because they are said to be pleasant, quiet and devout. I always expected the Devil to be at work and thought he would not do it through Papists. The Devil is stirring up this grievous division among our followers and us, but God will quickly trample him under our feet.

Martin Luther, letter to Melanchthon, January 13th 1522

Enquiries
Revolt in Germany

(a) Study Sources B and C

> Compare these Sources as evidence for the scale and nature of unrest in Germany in 1525

(b) Study all the Sources

> Use your own knowledge to assess how far the Sources support the interpretation that Luther was responsible for the Peasants Revolt in 1525

Source A: Luther sympathises with peasant grievances but at the same time urges restraint and order.

Dear friends, I admit it to be said (sad to say!) all too true and certain that the princes and lords, who forbid the preaching of the Gospel and oppress the people so unbearably, have well deserved that God put them down from their seats as men who have sinned deeply against God and man. Nevertheless, you must have a care that you take up your cause with a good conscience and with justice.

Luther, *Admonition to Peace*, April 1525

Source B: A radical leader of the Peasants Revolt calls on his supporters to continue the rebellion.

The whole of Germany, France and the Roman lands are awake. At Fulda four churches were destroyed. The peasants in Klettgau and Hergau are up, three thousand strong, and the longer it goes on the more they are. So now On! On! On! – it is time to hunt down the knaves like dogs. Have no mercy. Do not look at the misery of the Godless. Get going in the villages and towns, and especially with the miners and other good fellows. You shall not be put off by the numbers against you, for it is not your battle but God's.

Thomas Müntzer, an open letter to his followers, April 1525

Source C: A chronicler reports on the unrest in southern Germany during the Peasants Revolt.

Through certain citizens in this town who hold to the heresy of Luther, false teaching has greatly got the upper hand, owing to the deceit and concessions of some of the town authorities (21 March 1525). Thirty or forty peasants got together in a mob and marched upon the town (24 March). Someone has knocked off the head of Christ's image on a crucifix and struck off arms (20 April). The women run up and down with forks and sticks, declaring that they will plunder all the priests' houses, but are prevented. The citizens are summoned to decide whether they will aid the peasants. The majority decide to send them guns and pikes, powder and lead.

A contemporary chronicle, March-April 1525

Source D: Luther denounces the peasants.

In the third place they cloak this terrible and horrible sin with the Gospel, call themselves Christian Brethren, receive oaths and homage and compel people to hold with them to these abominations. Thus they become the greatest of all blasphemers of God and slanderers of his holy Name, serving the Devil, under the outward appearance of the Gospel, thus earning death in body and soul ten times over.

Martin Luther, *Against the Murdering, Thieving Hordes of Peasants*, May 1525

Source E: Luther reflects on the Peasants Revolt.

What an outcry I have caused with my little pamphlet against the peasants! Everything God has done for the world through me is forgotten. Now lords, priests and peasants are all against me and threaten me with death.

Since they are so frantic and foolish, I will prepare myself to be found, when my end comes, in the state that God created me. This should make my enemies even more frantic and foolish before the final farewell.

Luther, a letter to his friends, June 1525

The role of the princes after 1530 is important for **Key Issue 4** (see page iv).

KEY PERSON

Albrecht of Hohenzollern (1490–1568) Albrecht of Hohenzollern became grand master of the Teutonic Knights in 1511. The order nominally ruled over East Prussia which brought Albrecht into conflict with the crown of Poland, culminating in a war which began in December 1519 and devastated Prussia. Albrecht was granted a four-year truce early in 1521. The dispute was referred to Emperor Charles V and other princes, but no settlement was reached. Albrecht continued his efforts to obtain help in anticipation of a renewal of the war. For this purpose he visited the Diet of Nuremberg in 1522, where he made the acquaintance of the reformer Andreas Osiander, by whose influence Albrecht was won over to Protestantism. The Grand Master then journeyed to Wittenberg, where he was advised by Luther to abandon the rules of his Order, to marry, and to convert Prussia into a hereditary duchy for himself. In doing so Albrecht became the first German duke of Prussia. In imperial politics Albrecht was fairly active. Joining the League of Torgau in 1526, he acted in unison with the Protestants, and was among the princes who banded together to overthrow Charles V after the issue of the Augsburg Interim in May 1548. For various reasons, however, poverty and personal inclination among others, he did not take a prominent part in the military operations of this period.

CHAPTER 4

How did Lutheranism consolidate and expand?

THE POLITICAL CONTEXT OF THE GERMAN REFORMATION

Introduction

It became apparent to Luther after the Peasants' Revolt of 1525 that the guidance and direction for reform had to come from the princes. In Luther's mind the princes owed their position of authority to God, and as a result it was their duty to oversee reform. Moreover, if the Lutheran movement was going to survive and expand in the years after the Edict of Worms of 1521 (see page 41), then it was going to need the support and protection of the princes.

The attitude of the princes

Although the princes were initially unwilling to commit themselves totally to the Lutheran cause, generally for fear that the movement might be short lived and collapse, as time passed more and more territorial lords threw their lot in with Luther. Princes embraced reform for a variety of reasons:

- Some princes were committed Lutherans, such as Philip of Hesse or John of Saxony.
- Some were pressurised by the local populace into adopting Lutheranism, such as the Archbishop of Mainz at Erfurt.
- Others wished greater freedom from Habsburg authority, such as the Palatinate or Anhalt Dessau.
- Moreover, the material benefits of reform could be great as the secularisation of Church lands brought greater revenue and power, as shown by **Albrecht of Hohenzollern**, the first prince to support Luther.

Princely support was therefore crucial to the survival and consolidation of Lutheranism. After 1525, princely support became more committed and organised in the form of military, defensive leagues, the most significant being the Schmalkaldic League. By 1555, over half of Germany was ruled by Lutheran princes.

The search for unity, 1530–55

From 1530 onwards it became clear that warfare was inevitable, as two armed camps had emerged, based on religion. The main aim of imperial policy was to find a solution that would restore religious unity. In 1541, Charles V still believed, 24 years after the Luther affair began, that a doctrinal compromise between Catholicism and Protestantism could be found. In retrospect, this was naïve, as Lutheranism had laid down strong foundations and compromise over religious doctrine was unlikely. Charles V's absence from the Empire lessened his chances of success and, although a military victory was achieved over the Lutherans at Mühlberg on his return in 1547 (see page 84), the fact that he was unable to enforce Catholicism upon the populace demonstrates that Lutheranism was embedded within Germany. The Religious Peace of Augsburg in 1555 (see page 85) declared what many had felt inevitable for some time, but which had been unthinkable for Charles V – a bi-confessional Germany.

The implementation of the Edict of Worms

The rapid expansion of Lutheranism in the cities and then in the countryside took place in the face of the Edict of Worms (see page 41), which had outlawed Luther and banned his books. Indeed, the Edict was largely ignored by those cities and states intent on reform. The relative political autonomy of the princes and the cities, especially in the south of Germany, allowed Lutheranism to be adopted in safety. Charles V left behind a regency council after the Diet of Worms, which was headed by his brother Ferdinand, but it was weak, lacking in resources and the will to enforce the Edict of Worms effectively. Towns such as Hamburg and Nuremberg abandoned the Catholic Mass and printed Luther's work openly, and without any real fear of retribution. After all, **Ferdinand of Austria** could not risk major civil unrest.

KEY PEOPLE

Ferdinand of Austria was Charles V's younger brother and had been entrusted by Charles with the ruling of the Empire while Charles was in conflict with France. In 1522, Ferdinand had made an alliance with the two Dukes of Bavaria and the Bishop of Southern Germany in the hope of checking the spread of Lutheranism. The two brothers fell out in 1550 over who would succeed Ferdinand as Emperor. Charles proposed his son Philip, while Ferdinand promoted his son Maximilian. A compromise was reached, whereby Philip would succeed his father, and thereafter the succession would alternate between the two lines. Ultimately, the princes were so annoyed by this private settlement that enough pressure was brought to bear on Philip to renounce his succession, and Maximilian II took over in 1564.

The lack of central control is clearly demonstrated by the three Imperial Diets, which met at Nuremberg between 1521 and 1524. A strict enforcement of imperial policy was impossible given the political power and independence of the princes. Without any central control to enforce the Edict of Worms, those princes who wished to root out Lutheranism and defend Catholicism were forced to do so on their own initiative. In 1524, the regency council was dissolved and the Catholic League of Regensburg was established under the authority of Ferdinand of Austria and the Duke of Bavaria, along with the spiritual backing of the south German bishops. Further evidence that the Catholic princes were willing to take matters into their own hands came in 1525 when the League of Dessau was created, headed by Duke George of Saxony. These organised groupings demonstrated that imperial policy would have to be implemented through force, and this was unlikely to happen given that this period witnessed the greatest expansion of Lutheranism. However, the fact that warfare did not commence until the mid-1540s demonstrates that Charles believed a peaceful solution to the religious division in Germany could be found. Indeed, Charles urged Ferdinand to negotiate with the papacy and call a **General Council of the Church** at which the situation in Germany could be discussed and, hopefully, defused through reform from within the Catholic Church.

Torgau and Speyer
In response, the Lutherans, led by Philip of Hesse (see page 81), formed the rival League of Torgau in 1526, intent on ensuring that the Edict of Worms would not be enforced. Therefore, one can see a pattern emerging, which would hold for the next 20 years:

- Imperial policy was to find a compromise and restore unity.
- Yet, in the meantime, the lack of central imperial control and the absence of Charles V meant that the spread of Lutheranism could not be stopped.

Partly as a consequence, two rival groups emerged and, as time passed and compromise became increasingly unlikely, war appeared inevitable. However, while the possibility of negotiations existed, Charles instructed Ferdinand to play for time. The Diet of Speyer in 1526 was a good example of this tactic. It was most conciliatory towards the emerging religion. The Diet declared the following:

- The Edict of Worms would be implemented as each thought right before God and his imperial majesty. In short, the princes could interpret the edict as they wished. Effectively, toleration had been granted, and this declaration unquestionably gave Lutheranism the time and space necessary to consolidate its early gains.
- Church lands that had already been taken were to remain secularised.
- Over the next three years, Lutheranism developed in a secure environment and further towns embraced reform, while more princes joined the likes of Albrecht of Hohenzollern and Philip of Hesse in the defence of Lutheranism.

Charles acts against Lutheranism

Given this temporary period of toleration, one might have expected greater organisation of Lutherans along military lines, yet Luther himself condemned armed resistance to higher authorities and most princes heeded his decree. Charles V was determined to overturn the Speyer legislation as quickly as he could and in 1529 he was in a position to do so; his quarrel with France had been settled by the Treaty of Cambrai. The second Diet of Speyer in 1529 saw the 1526 decree overturned: no more Church land was to be secularised and the Edict of Worms was once more to be enforced strictly. This was a setback for the Lutheran princes, and demonstrated Charles V's ultimate commitment to one faith within the Empire; through negotiation or force. Yet, for Charles, the problem remained how to enforce the Edict of Worms effectively. The aggressive declaration at Speyer in 1529 was met with an aggressive response from the Lutheran princes.

- Six princes and fourteen imperial cities made a collective stand against Charles V, issuing a Protestation against the 1529 legislation.
- The commitment of the Lutheran princes to the Word of God was increasing and the stakes in this religious

The Marburg Colloquy, 1529 In order to try to present a united Protestant front against Habsburg aggression, Philip of Hesse invited important Protestant theological and political figures from Switzerland and Germany to his castle at Marburg. Luther, Melanchthon, Myconius, Zwingli, Bucer, Oecolampadius, Bullinger and Osiander made up a celebrated *Who's Who* of European reformers. Yet agreement and consensus could not be reached, with the primary stumbling-block being the Eucharist. Luther famously scrawled the contentious phrase in chalk on the table in front of Zwingli – *Hoc est corpus meum* (This is my body). For Luther there was a bodily transformation of bread and wine, but not so for Zwingli. The attempt to bring Protestant strands together had failed.

The Confession of Augsburg, 1530 Drafted by Melanchthon and signed by Elector John of Saxony, George of Brandenburg and the imperial city of Nuremberg among others, the *Confessio Augustana* was an attempt to define what the Lutheran Church believed, while still leaving the door open for reconciliation with the Catholic Church. Ultimately, while the document tried to highlight areas of agreement and even pampered Charles V by praising his war against the Turks, the gap between Lutheranism and Catholicism was unbridgeable. For example, Article 4 rejected the idea that through human effort forgiveness could be attained, while Article 20 stated that only through faith could salvation be gained. Article 22 espoused communion in both kinds and Article 24 attacked the idea of sacrifice in the Mass. In short, even while glossing over contentious issues there was little chance of the Emperor's agreeing to this document. Indeed, he endorsed the aggressive Catholic response entitled the *Confutatio*, drafted by Cardinal Campeggio. The Augsburg Confession survived, however, as the legal definition of Lutheranism. It was subscribed to by members of the Schmalkaldic League and used in the 1555 Peace of Augsburg. All of this despite the fact that Luther declared himself thoroughly displeased with such a shallow and conciliatory outline of Lutheranism.

conflict were being raised. The protesters, from whom we derive the term Protestant, were openly challenging imperial authority, answering to God not Emperor.

The Diet of Augsburg, 1530

Nevertheless, Charles V appeared to be in a strong position in 1529. The Recess of 1526 had been rescinded while, in 1529, the Lutheran movement appeared to be showing signs of division: Luther denounced the Swiss reformer Huldrych Zwingli at the **Marburg Colloquy**, thereby ensuring a split within Protestantism. Moreover, the situation in eastern Europe and Italy appeared favourable for Charles V – so much so that the Emperor was able to turn his attentions fully to Germany in 1530. Charles travelled to the Diet of Augsburg with the aim of restoring unity within the Church, while also enlisting German aid for the ongoing struggle against the Ottoman Turks. Furthermore, Charles wanted princely approval for his brother Ferdinand's nomination to be King of the Romans, a position that would make Ferdinand the heir to the imperial throne. Therefore, in some ways, we can still note a conflict of interests for Charles at the Diet of Augsburg. Perhaps it was the need to court the German princes that led to Charles seeking a theological compromise. Theologians from both the Catholic and Protestant camps were invited to attend the Diet yet, realistically, there was little chance of reaching a compromise.

The Augsburg Confession

It was Luther's young deputy Philip Melanchthon who prepared the Lutheran statement of belief known as the **Confession of Augsburg**. The confession was drafted from the Schwabach Articles which had been compiled by Luther in the summer of 1529, shortly before the Marburg Colloquy. The Augsburg Confession aimed to define Lutheranism and at the same time to reassure Catholic powers that the movement was not heretical and actually not terribly different from their own faith.

In this respect the context of the Diet of Augsburg becomes important. In the immediate wake of the failure of Protestant unity at Marburg and the imminent return of Charles V to the Empire, the confession was an attempt to distinguish Lutheranism from other more radical sects and to protect a movement which was looking rather vulnerable.

Luther, as an outlaw under the Edict of Worms, was not allowed to attend the Diet, and for his own safety he was confined to the castle of Feste Coburg for six months. Melanchthon was more open to a spirit of compromise with the Catholics than Luther, and he had high hopes that some form of reconciliation could be reached between Lutherans and moderate Catholics.

- Melanchthon deliberately avoided contentious issues in the Confession of Augsburg, such as purgatory and transubstantiation, in the hope of reaching a compromise with the Catholic theologians led by Albert of Mainz.
- Melanchthon focused instead on doctrinal issues such as communion in both kinds and clerical marriage, on which he hoped Catholic moderates might agree with him.

Yet no matter how far Melanchthon tried to make Lutheranism acceptable to Catholic deputies, he was unlikely to succeed. Hard-line Catholics around the Emperor, such as the papal representative Campeggio, focused on the differences between the two faiths rather than the similarities. Melanchthon's draft had obviously stressed the centrality of justification by faith alone and questioned papal supremacy, two issues which the Catholic theologians were not going simply to ignore. The confession was submitted to the Diet on 25th June 1530. On the Catholic side, Charles V instructed Johannes Eck to draft a reply which was known as the Confutation. This document pulled out the key differences between Catholicism and Lutheranism, and did little to promote a sense of unity. Indeed, once the Confutation had been accepted by the Emperor, it was clear that the Diet of Augsburg would not result in a settlement between the two faiths.

Consequences of the Diet of Augsburg 1530

- Lutherans abandoned the search for a compromise with Catholics, and reconciliation was impossible as a result.
- Lutheranism now had a document which defined its doctrinal position. This served to differentiate the movement not only from Catholicism but also from other Protestant faiths.
- In the final decree of the Diet of Augsburg, Charles V reaffirmed the Edict of Worms and gave Protestants until April 1531 to return to the Catholic fold, after which time they would be subject to armed and legal measures.
- The battle lines were effectively drawn between the two faiths, and, as a consequence of failure at Augsburg, religious war appeared imminent.
- Luther also gave his personal approval to the suggestion of resisting the Emperor by force, on the grounds that Charles had contravened God's will.
- Lutheran princes organised themselves into a formal military alliance known as the Schmalkaldic League.

The Schmalkaldic League, 1530–43

Charles' aggressive decree after Augsburg, combined with the stated re-affirmation of the Edict of Worms, prompted a predictable response from the Lutheran princes. In 1531, a princely alliance was formed at the town of Schmalkalden, led by Philip of Hesse (see page 81) and including the princes of Anhalt, Mansfeld, Braunschweig–Lüneburg and the Elector of Saxony. Eleven imperial cities also joined the league in 1531, including Strasburg, Ulm and Bremen. The importance of the Schmalkaldic League should not be underestimated:

- The League represented the most formal and organised opposition to imperial power up to this point. Not only were its members agreeing to help each other should they be attacked on account of the word of God and the doctrine of the Gospel, they were also renouncing their membership from all imperial institutions.
- For the first time, a group of princes was operating outside the recognised political structure of the Empire, and the theory that the emperor could not be opposed by force was being challenged.

- Even Luther insisted that, if a war broke out, those who opposed murderers and bloodthirsty papists would be acting in self-defence against an unjust force.

Protestant interests now had a powerful backing, and the empire was clearly divided into two armed camps.

Peace of Nuremberg, 1532

Unsurprisingly, the Schmalkaldic League received backing from the French king, Francis I, eager to exploit divisions within the Empire and hinder the progress of Charles V. Moreover, Charles' continuing problem with the Ottoman Empire meant that he had to compromise his position once more in 1532. The Religious Peace of Nuremberg

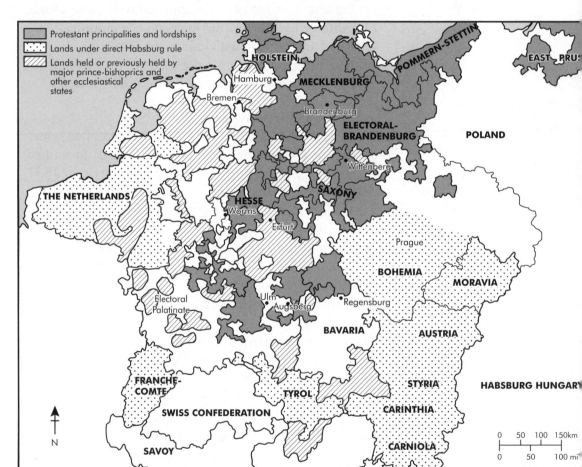

German principalities on the eve of the Schmalkaldic War, c.1547.

Duke Ulrich of Württemberg (1487–1550) In 1511, Ulrich of Wurttemberg was married to Sabina, daughter of Albert IV Duke of Bavaria and niece of the emperor, Maximilian. The marriage was an unhappy one, and Ulrich developed an affection for the wife of Hans von Hutten, a kinsman of Ulrich von Hutten. In 1515, Ulrich von Württemberg killed Hans von Hutten during an altercation, and a series of events unfolded. Sabina fled from her husband seeking support from the emperor, her uncle, and her brother William IV, Duke of Bavaria. Ulrich was twice placed under the imperial ban, and, following the death of the emperor in January 1519, the Swabian League drove Ulrich from Württemberg.

Württemberg was occupied by Austrian forces during the 1520s. Ulrich was an early convert to Lutheranism, and, in 1534, his confessional loyalties gained him the support of the Schmalkaldic League and its leader, Philip of Hesse. The league was strengthened by support from Francis I, and invaded Württemberg in April 1534. Charles V and his brother Ferdinand I were able to offer only limited support to their lieutenants, and the Austrian Habsburg troops were finally defeated at Lauffen on May 13th. Ulrich was restored within a matter of weeks, and was recognised as a duke by Ferdinand under a treaty negotiated at Kadan in June 1534.

gained him men and money for the fight against the Ottoman leader Suleiman, but conceded toleration to the Protestants until a General Council could be called at which the split could be discussed and, in Charles' eyes, healed. This toleration, combined with the fact that, between 1533 and 1542, Charles was not in Germany, once more allowed Lutheranism the chance to lay down firm foundations under the protection of the League. The expansion was not like that of the 1520s – dramatic, urban and revolutionary – but gradual and encompassing large expanses of territory. The power of the League was clearly demonstrated in 1534 when **Duke Ulrich** was restored to his Duchy of Württemberg at the expense of the Habsburgs. Aided by French financial backing, the League forced Ferdinand and Charles to recognise Duke Ulrich as the rightful ruler, and the victory displayed the strength of the League to other princes, who now felt confident enough to join up.

The long road to war

The Lutheran cause received a further boost in 1536, when the **Wittenberg Concord** ensured unity among the German Protestant states. At the heart of this unity was agreement about the nature of the Eucharist. The inevitable road towards war was also further underlined in 1537, when the **Schmalkalden Articles** justified resistance to the emperor in the cause of the word of God. The 1530s ended, however, without such a war taking place. The preoccupation of Charles with Francis I and Suleiman, combined with the strength of the League and the inability of the papacy to summon a General Council of the Church, meant that Protestantism continued to expand. Indeed, in 1541 at Regensburg Charles appeared to be repeating the same mistakes of the Diet of Augsburg in 1530.

THE COLLOQUY OF REGENSBURG 1541

Why did Charles seek a negotiated settlement with the Lutherans at Regensburg in 1541?

In 1538 Charles V concluded the truce of Nice with France, which freed up time, money and resources for Germany. Charles V's ongoing imperial concerns also contrived to save Protestantism from a major Catholic offensive. Rebellion in Ghent in 1539 occupied a sizeable army, as well as Charles himself. In that same year a crisis emerged in the duchy of Cleves on the Lower Rhine. The death of Duke John meant that his son William came to the throne. William also inherited the territories of Julich and Berg from his mother. A year earlier he had also successfully laid claim to the strategically important state of Guelders. These lands combined created a power bloc in north-west Germany which threatened Habsburg supply routes between Italy and the Netherlands. Cleves was not Lutheran, but neither did it owe much allegiance to Rome. The Duke was head of both Church and state, and this new rogue state in the north was a considerable problem for Charles. Action against the Protestants could not be contemplated until the threat of Cleves had been neutralised. In 1539 William opened negotiations with the Schmalkaldic League, and one year later married off his sister Anne to Henry VIII. A general alliance of England, the League and Cleves looked a distinct possibility in 1540, but the plan quickly collapsed. Henry found Anne of Cleves unsuitable and William realised that he was better served by an alliance with France. Matters came to a head in 1543 when William was defeated by the Emperor, losing Guelders in the process.

Given the circumstances of 1539–40, Charles decided to fall back on the trusted policy of conciliation and to that end it was agreed to hold discussions between theologians from both religious parties in order to reach a doctrinal compromise. The strategy had failed at Augsburg in 1530, and was unlikely to succeed in 1541 because the same key differences between the two faiths persisted. Charles's continued policy of reunion by negotiation, however, highlights his reluctance to go to war. Charles sought a negotiated settlement with the Protestants before the structure of the Catholic Church collapsed entirely. War was a last resort for Charles, which explains why the conference of Catholic and Protestant representatives, planned in 1539, finally took place in 1541 at Regensburg.

What happened at Regensburg in 1541?

- Pope Paul III sent Gasparo Contarini to lead the Catholic delegation. In doing so he knew he was sending a liberal theologian capable of healing the rift with the German Protestants. Cardinal Contarini was a key figure in the Catholic Reformation, belonging to the Oratory of Divine Love. Contarini was in many ways the ideal man for Regensburg, as he had some sympathy for the Lutheran belief in justification by faith alone. He belonged to a distinguished group of Catholic reformers who became known as the *spirituali*. Contarini, like Luther, drew heavily upon the teachings and ideas of St Augustine. Doctrinal orthodoxy within the Catholic Church was still to be achieved, and Contarini's outlook showed the broad range of beliefs that existed. Of course Contarini's loyalty to Rome rather stood him apart from Luther. Contarini was supported by the chancellor of Cologne, John Gropper, another moderate Catholic reformer.

- Just as at Augsburg in 1530, the Protestant leader was Philip Melanchthon. Melanchthon's credentials as one of the leading intellectual figures of the Protestant Reformation were already secure, and he remained the one figure capable of attaining religious unity. Melanchthon was backed by Martin Bucer, another Protestant committed to finding a middle ground with Catholicism.

- Hopes of a lasting settlement were raised when, within weeks, agreement was reached on the first five articles of the draft agreement, The Book of Regensburg. A joint definition of justification was achieved to the amazement of many onlookers. The successful formula enshrined the principle of double justification. This satisfied moderate Catholics because it maintained the role of good works, whilst moderate Lutherans were appeased by the idea that faith was the key to salvation.

- Doctrinal agreement was short lived, however, because both Luther and the papacy denounced double justification. Luther was critical of Melanchthon for giving in to Catholic pressure over good works, whilst Pope Paul III was reluctant to make any doctrinal concessions to the Protestants at this stage. In short, agreements at Regensburg had been put together by moderate idealists, whilst the real decision makers were hard-line dogmatists.

- That said, there was no guarantee that even the moderates at Regensburg would reach agreement. A middle ground had been found over the first five articles, but progress was less visible over the remaining eighteen points of doctrine. The old issues of papal supremacy and transubstantiation continued to provide obstacles to conciliation and, like all previous attempts to find religious unity, Regensburg ended in total failure.

The Consequences of Failure

- On the Catholic side, Regensburg represented something of a watershed. As a result of the failure of conciliation, a new course was marked out by the creation of the Roman Inquisition in July 1541. The spirit of reconciliation embraced by the *spirituali* was over, and the emergence of the Inquisition in Italy heralded a new era in the defence of Catholicism from the threat of Protestantism.
- On the Protestant side, Regensburg illustrated once more Luther's reluctance to compromise his doctrinal position. Luther sincerely believed that his ideas were the truth; were God's Word. Luther put matters of faith ahead of matters of policy at Regensburg, just as he had done at Augsburg a decade before, and this left no room for conciliation. Luther was also facing another major trial at this time relating to Philip of Hesse (see page 81).
- For Charles, the 1530s had been frustrating in that other political concerns had prevented him from addressing the Lutheran problem. He may have sincerely sought religious compromise but in his heart must have known that Lutheranism had developed to such an extent that finding a middle ground was unlikely and perhaps unrealistic. At least Charles could find solace in the fact that his favoured means of resolving the religious dispute, namely a General Council of the Church, was finally going to become a reality. After years of procrastination by the Papacy, a General Council was summoned by Paul III to meet in 1542. The Council would eventually open in the town of Trent in December 1545.

Charles re-entered Germany in 1543 for only the third time in his imperial life. A year previously, the last remaining Catholic prince in the north, Duke Henry of Brunswick–Wolfenbüttel, had been driven out by the League. Therefore, potential support for Charles in the north of Germany was thin on the ground. Charles would remain in Germany for twelve years and depart a broken and defeated man, leaving behind him an empire in which Catholic and Protestant states coexisted.

DIVIDE AND RULE 1543–8

Opportunity for the Habsburgs

On Charles' return, however, the situation was looking brighter for a Habsburg reconquest of Lutheran gains. Indeed, there were signs that the Schmalkaldic League was beginning to crack:

- In 1541, **Philip of Hesse** was exposed as a bigamist and, worse still, Luther had given him the authority to marry again. Hesse had to plead for his life before the emperor, as bigamy was a crime punishable by death. He was pardoned but, as a political force, he was ruined.
- Furthermore, the defeat of France in 1544 removed foreign aid to the League and freed Charles to concentrate on Germany. The Turkish threat in Hungary came to nothing and, with papal help assured, Charles could set about breaking the League.
- With war on the horizon and the diplomatic position favouring Charles, Martin Luther died on 18 February 1546, aged 63. By this time, he had become rather impatient and cantankerous, scornful of those who did not agree with his doctrinal position. Perhaps such stubbornness prevented a unification between various strands of Protestantism, yet one cannot underestimate his significant achievements.

DIET OF REGENSBURG 1546

In April 1546 Charles V travelled to Regensburg to attend one final religious colloquy. Unlike in 1541 there was no sincere attempt to attain religious unity, and there was little theological debate. Charles V's main priority was to finalize his alliance with Maurice of Saxony and prepare a defensive pact with Bavaria in readiness for war.

The Policy of Charles V after Regensburg: 1541–7

- Charles V realised after 1541 that the religious problem in Germany could only be resolved by force. To this end he set about a dual policy of outward conciliation with the Protestants in order to secure aid for the ongoing war against France, while also building up a power bloc amongst the princes in preparation for a military strike. Charles V's successful campaign against the Duke of Cleves in 1543 demonstrates the increase in imperial power at this stage in proceedings as Charles sought to turn back advances made in the previous two decades. Duke William was forced to accept the Treaty of Venloo in which he promised to restore Catholicism in his territories.
- The Peace of Crepy (1544) with France marked an important turning point for Charles as it allowed him to focus his resources entirely upon the German lands. It also neutralised the threat of French support for the German Protestants. By 1545 Charles had collected troops from the Netherlands, Hungary and Italy and mobilised them for a decisive strike against the heretics. Papal support was also secured in 1545, which comes as something of a surprise given the dire relations between Paul III and Charles V over the course of the Habsburg Valois Wars since 1541. Charles was able to win over papal assistance on the basis that Rome was eager to see a decisive strike against heresy in the Empire and a restoration of their authority there. The opening of a General Council of the Church at Trent in 1545 also heralded a new era of Catholic renewal and reform. A formal alliance was concluded in June 1546 by which papal troops would assist Charles in the destruction of heresy in German lands.
- In 1542, Charles V's task of turning back the Reformation in the Empire was enormous. All northern Germany was Protestant by this stage and there were signs that the bishoprics of Cologne and Munster were also considering reform. Hermann von Wied, the Archbishop Elector of Cologne, asked Martin Bucer and

Melanchthon to help him initiate a programme of spiritual reform. Ultimately Charles V's victory over Duke William of Cleves would ensure that Colgne's flirtation with reform was relatively brief. That said, another elector, this time Frederick II of the Palatinate, also began to befriend the Schmalkaldic League in 1546, and allowed Lutheran preachers into his territories.

- Charles pursued a skilful diplomatic policy in the Holy Roman Empire between 1544–6, and built up a series of alliances with important princes. A pact with Bavaria was secured through the proposed marriage of Ferdinand's eldest daughter to Duke Albert's eldest son. Charles was not afraid to use the self-interest and ambition of princes to court support. Importantly, Charles was able to win over the Protestant Duke Maurice of Saxony with the promise that the electoral title would be his in return for military assistance. Maurice was from the junior Albertine branch of the Saxon family, which was effectively excluded from the electoral title after an agreement in 1485 which had given it over to the senior Ernestine line. The carrot of a grand title, and with it great power, was too much for Maurice to resist.

- Charles V was aided by the weaknesses of the Schmalkaldic League at the very time it needed to be at its strongest. The League was slow to recognise Charles V's policy of divide and rule within the Empire, and failed to see the powerful alliance that was being deployed against them. The leadership of the Schmalkaldic League was dealt a major blow in 1541 when Philip of Hesse was exposed as a bigamist. Worse still, Luther had given him the authority to marry again. Hesse had to plead for his life before the Emperor as bigamy was a capital crime punishable by death. Hesse was pardoned and even returned to head the league in 1544, but was ruined in terms of his political reputation. Not all reformed territories belonged to the League, as political concerns dictated that important states such as Brandenburg remained with the military alliance. The Margrave of Brandenburg felt the League was simply a vehicle to drive the selfish policies of Hesse and Saxony. Charles V exploited the young Margrave John of Brandenburg-Kustrin's political concerns about the growing power of Saxony. Together with Maurice and the Margrave Albert Alcibades of Brandenburg-Culmbach, John of Kustrin made up a triumvirate of young princes with little affiliation to the religious struggle who could act as a counter weight to the Schmalkaldic League.

Conclusion of the Diet of Regensburg

By 1546 Charles had built up a powerful coalition of forces against the League. The League, for its part, appeared isolated and vulnerable. Although the pretence of another religious colloquy was maintained at the Diet of Regensburg in 1546, Charles was unable to disguise the meeting as anything more than a final effort to pull together alliances with Maurice and Bavaria. The anticipated war began in 1546, and it did not last long once Charles V's troops arrived from the Netherlands and Italy. In October, Maurice demonstrated his new loyalties with an attack on Ernestine Saxony. Several cities along the Danube were taken with relative ease by Charles although the Reformation was only overturned in Augsburg. The decisive battle took place at Mühlberg in Saxony in April 1547. Despite their numerical advantage (the Schmalkaldic force numbered 80,000 in comparison with the imperial army of 56,000) the Protestants were no match for the experienced and well equipped Spanish troops of Charles V. The result was a crushing victory for Charles V. John Frederick, the Elector of Saxony, was captured along with Philip of Hesse. As promised, the Ernestine lands and title were handed over to Maurice. The League crumbled, and it appeared that Germany was firmly in the hands of Charles V.

The Battle of Mühlberg, 1547

Charles continued to clear the way for war, luring Maurice of Saxony and the Margrave of Brandenburg to his side through bribery and promises of power. Such young princes who had no grounding in the origins of the religious schism were easily won over, yet their defection was a clear sign that the powerful League of the 1530s had disappeared. The crucial battle came in 1547 at Mühlberg in Saxony. Despite having a numerical advantage (the Schmalkaldic force numbered 80,000 in comparison to the

KEY ISSUES

The Schmalkaldic War of 1547 is important for **Key Issue 4** (see page iv).

imperial force of 56,000), the Schmalkaldic army was no match for the experienced and well-equipped Spanish troops of Charles V. The result was a crushing victory for Charles V. John Frederick, the Elector of Saxony, was captured and, as promised, his lands were turned over to Maurice. The League crumbled and it appeared that all of Germany was in the hands of Charles V.

The Diet of Augsburg, 1547–8

Yet such a victory as that at Mühlberg did not mean that Charles could impose his Catholic will upon the populace. Lutheranism was too strong at grass-roots level for any Catholic decree to be observed. Many German towns had been worshipping in a Lutheran manner for the past 20 years. The resulting Diet of Augsburg in 1547–8 proved this point:

- Charles laid out plans for a strengthening of central government, something which the princes never enjoyed hearing, as their privileges and traditions would be compromised.
- An Augsburg Interim (1548) was drawn up which gave few concessions to Lutheranism and effectively formed a Catholic statement of belief, which was to be observed by all cities and states in the Empire. The Interim was to be imperial law until a General Council of the Church decided upon matters of doctrine.

The Augsburg Interim represented a lost chance for Charles to introduce a realistic and workable peace settlement to the population of Germany. Yet one would expect little else from a man as set in his ways as Charles V. He had strived all his imperial life for a unity based upon the doctrine of Catholicism. He was unlikely to abandon such principles now, especially after a great military victory. Yet the Interim was largely ignored by the princes and city magistrates of the Empire, and Charles did not have the means to enforce it.

KEY ISSUES

The Peace of Augsburg 1555 is important for **Key Issue 4** (see page iv).

The Peace of Augsburg, 1555

Charles' attempts to enforce a moderate re-Catholicisation of the Empire were only successful in those areas where his army was present. Moreover, the Habsburg family itself was

showing signs of strain as Charles sought to promote his
son Philip to the imperial throne after his death, at the
expense of Ferdinand. Such disunity was seized upon by
the young Maurice, newly-entitled Elector of Saxony.
Charles' policy of divide and rule backfired as the maverick
young Maurice led a sizeable army south, boosted by
French aid, in a bid to free his father-in-law Philip of Hesse
and gain the city of Magdeburg, thereby consolidating his
electoral title. This revolt forced Charles to flee into
Carinthia and leave his brother to negotiate the
humiliating **Treaty of Passau** in 1552.

Charles was entirely disenchanted by the events that had
followed the victory at Mühlberg. Moreover, his financial
position had steadily deteriorated; years of warfare and
religious strife had taken their toll both physically and
materially. By 1555, all religious matters of the empire
were in the hands of Ferdinand. Finally, at Augsburg, a
pragmatic and workable solution was found whereby
Catholicism and Lutheranism were allowed to coexist
within the Empire:

- Notably, it was the prince of each territory who decided
  upon the religion of its inhabitants. Therefore, the
  political autonomy of the princes was effectively
  recognised. On the back of the Reformation their power
  and influence had increased.

**Luther with the
reformers. To the right
of Luther are
Bugenhagen, Erasmus
(included for his
scholarly
achievements), Jonas,
Cruziger and
Melanchthon. Spalatin
and Forster stand to
Luther's left. Copy
after Lucas Cranach
the Younger.**

John Calvin (1509–64) was twenty-six years younger than Luther, and is often seen as leading the second wave of Protestant reform in Europe. Between 1538–64 Calvin gave Protestantism an institutional structure and he worked tirelessly to mould a reformed city in Geneva and to spread his doctrinal message further afield. Calvin's doctrine was similar in many ways to that of Luther although he put a greater emphasis on predestination, arguing that God had chosen both those to be saved and those to be damned. Calvinism made a great impact both in Calvin's homeland of France and in the Netherlands.

- The crucial decree within the **Religious Peace of Augsburg** was *cuius regio, eius religio*. In short, he who ruled the principality would decree its religion.
- Emigration was the answer for those committed Catholics who found themselves in a Lutheran state or vice versa. Yet, in reality, the Peace merely recognised what had been the situation on the ground for the previous two decades.
- Importantly, the Peace specifically mentioned Lutheranism, and no freedom of worship was to be granted to any other form of religion. More radical groups such as the Anabaptists were not recognised and, more importantly, there was no mention of Calvinism. The year 1555 also marked **John Calvin's** triumph in Geneva and the international impact of that faith was perhaps more marked and widespread than that of Lutheranism.

Indeed, although the Religious Peace of Augsburg remained intact for the next 63 years, the second wave of reform initiated by Calvin and the growing Catholic response meant that religious strife in Europe had only just begun.

CONCLUSION

It is clear, therefore, that the spectacular successes of Lutheranism in the 1520s were consolidated by the princes after 1530:

- Large territorial gains were made, but the movement lost its exuberant popular edge.
- Lutheranism became, for some princes, a vehicle for political power or material wealth. Indeed, one could argue that the movement failed to fulfil its early promise, and outside Germany and Scandinavia its gains were few.
- Co-operation and union with other Protestant groups, such as the Zwinglians, had proved impossible, diluting the overall challenge to Catholicism.
- Luther's energy and idealism of the early 1520s gave way to stubbornness and frustration.

The narrative of the German Reformation after 1530 can almost be told without mention of its figurehead. One could argue that Luther had always been a conservative reformer, yet the extent to which the movement had become politicised under the princes can be illustrated by the fact that, at Augsburg in 1555, they were given the decision on which faith to adopt. Luther had laid down his theology in the 1520s and, while he was still involved in church organisation, much of his work was being carried out by Melanchthon, Bugenhagen and others. Nevertheless, what had been unimaginable in 1500 had occurred by 1555: the people of the Empire could now choose between two Christian faiths.

ACTIVITY

1. How would you describe Luther's tone in Source 1?

2. Use your own knowledge to establish the context of Source 1. What was happening in 1520 which might make Luther eager to court princely support?

3. How can you explain the final line *It is a pity that kings and princes have so little reverence for Christ that they allow such wicked things to happen* which seems to be deeply critical of the very people that Luther is trying to attract?

Source 1

I should be very glad if kings, princes and all the nobles expelled the crooks from Rome from the country, and kept Church appointments out of their hands. Roman greed has seized all the Church offices in Germany. Who has ever heard of such monstrous robbery? Do we not also have the people who need these offices? In our poverty we must enrich the donkey-drivers and stable boys, even the harlots and crooks at Rome, who regards us as fools, and make us the objects of their vile mockery. It is a pity that kings and princes have so little reverence for Christ that they allow such wicked things to happen.

Martin Luther, *On the Papacy at Rome*, 1520

4. What does Source 2 tell us about the effectiveness of the Edict of Worms since 1521?

5. What does the line *Things have become so bad that the present mild approach needs to be stopped* in Source 2 tell us about the development of Lutheranism under princely support?

Source 2

The Edict of Worms issued at the Diet in 1521 must be obeyed. This is possible if the Emperor can be persuaded to carry out a vigorous policy. The laws on religion should not be changed at the new Diet of Speyer. Particular care should be taken to see if the Emperor can cancel the meeting. If this is not possible, the Diet should be delayed. The Pope should consider doing more about the Elector of Saxony. A lengthy report has been prepared about this, as the Pope ordered. Things have become so bad that the present mild approach needs to be stopped and the harsher penalties of the Church applied. John should be removed as an Imperial Elector.

Report of the Papal Curia, 1528

Enquiries
Luther and the Princes

(a) Study Sources B and E

Compare these sources as evidence for Charles V's difficulties in dealing with the Lutheran problem.

(b) Study all the Sources

> Use your own knowledge to assess how far the Sources support the interpretation that the success of Lutheranism depended entirely on the support of the princes.

Source A: The Venetian Ambassador highlights the importance of the princes to Luther's cause.

Luther will not give ground on an opinion even in the face of argument and threats. He has many powerful supporters among the princes who encourage and protect him. Nobody dares attack them. Although his books have been banned by the Pope and the Emperor – who is actually here – they are openly available here in Worms.

> Gasparo Contarini, the Venetian Ambassador
> in his report to the Venetian government, 1521

Source B: A Papal representative questions Frederick the Wise's involvement in Luther's disappearance.

We believe that Frederick, the Elector of Saxony, was involved in Luther's disappearance. The Emperor, all the other princes and virtually the whole Court thought this, so the Elector had to swear before the Diet that he knew nothing of this matter. However, one cannot trust him-especially when it comes to the question of Luther. Many people believe that the Elector wanted to get Luther into a place of safety before the Imperial safe conduct that Luther was given to attend the Diet had expired. He wanted to give the impression that others had arrested Luther, or murdered him.

> Jerome Aleander, Report to the Pope, 1521

Source C: Luther attacks the Pope.

It is a wicked fable that only the Pope can interpret the Bible. The Church authorities have seized this authority for themselves. Spiritual authority was not given only to the Pope but to the whole community. If we believe in the priesthood of all believers, should we not have the power to examine and decide what is right or wrong in religious matters? The Bible should make us free and bold, and the spirit of freedom should not be chased away by the inventions of the Pope.

Martin Luther, An Appeal to the Christian Nobility of the
German Nation, 1520

Source D: Luther comments on the importance of princely power and supports obedience to princes, described here as holders of the sword.

We must firmly establish secular power and the sword, that no one may doubt that it is in the world by God's will. Because the sword is a very great benefit and necessary to the whole world, to preserve peace, to punish sin and to prevent evil, a true Christian submits most willingly to the rule of the sword, pays taxes, honours those in authority, serves, helps and does all he can to further the government, that it may be held in honour and fear.

Luther, *Secular Authority: To
What Extent It Should be Obeyed*, 1522

Source E: A modern historian considers the reasons for the success of Lutheranism.

Modern historians have attached increasing importance to Luther's appeal to the imperial cities and town councils. By 1546 most of the 65 free cities and hundreds of smaller towns had adopted Lutheranism. Recent studies have shown that each urban group responded to Luther's theology with individuality and diversity. At Erfurt and Wittenberg, the role of preachers was vital in stimulating and controlling the pace and extent of reform; at Nuremberg and Ulm, the city councils implemented changes but only after a public debate and vote had been taken; and in Strasbourg, the town guilds played a decisive part.

Geoffrey Woodward, *The Sixteenth Century Reformation*, Hodder 2001

CHAPTER 5

What were Luther's views on other Protestants?

MARTIN BUCER AND THE REFORMATION IN STRASBURG

What was Martin Bucer's background?

Martin Bucer (1491–1551) entered the Dominican monastic order in 1506, from where he was sent to study at the University of Heidelberg, Germany. It was here that Bucer became familiar with the works of Christian Humanists such as Erasmus, as well as the ideas of Luther. He was soon converted to the new faith, and, in 1521, Bucer withdrew from the Dominican Order. One year later he found himself in the service of Count Palatinate of the Rhine, an Imperial Elector. Bucer became a pastor at Landstuhl where he married a former nun, Elisabeth Silbereisen. After his excommunication in 1523, Bucer made his way to Strasburg on the Upper Rhine. Strasburg was widely acknowledged as a centre for Christian humanism and religious exiles of all persuasions. Between the years 1523–48, Bucer would play a pivotal role in directing the course of the Reformation in southern Germany from his headquarters in Strasburg.

What was the nature of the Reformation in Strasburg?

In 1523 the city council of Strasburg appointed three reformed preachers in Bucer, Wolfgang Capito and Caspar Heido to work alongside the cathedral priest, Matthew Zell. The council moved cautiously at first as they did not want religious change to fuel civil unrest. Within five years the churches in the city had been cleansed of ornamentation and images while the Latin mass was abandoned in favour of a German service. Whilst Strasburg had clearly turned over to the Reformation, then, it was less clear whether the course of reform would be Lutheran or Zwinglian. Bucer's own theological position was more in line with that of Zwingli than Luther, especially on the question of the Lord's Supper (Bucer rejected the idea of the physical presence of Christ in the Eucharist). That said, Bucer was determined that doctrinal differences should not constitute an obstacle to unity between different strands of Protestantism. He constantly tried to mediate between the various confessional groups to find a middle ground, and was a prominent figure at the Colloquy of Marburg in 1529. Bucer's attempts to promote reconciliation at all costs prompted criticism from other parties who believed that he was too ready to compromise on serious doctrinal points. Frustrated by the lack of progress at Marburg he drew up his own confession of faith at the Diet of Augsburg in 1530, the *Confessio Tetrapolitina*, which Strasburg shared with Constance, Lindau and Memmingen.

How did Bucer's Reformation in Strasburg differ from that of Luther in Wittenberg?

The reformation in Strasburg followed its own unique course during the 1520s and 1530s. Although unquestionably influenced by both Lutheranism and Zwinglianism, the reformation in Strasburg was more liberal and accommodating. Under the direction of Bucer, attempts were made to pull together the different strands of Protestantism, including the more radical sects such as the Anabaptists.

In line with reformed Swiss cities, Strasburg placed a heavy emphasis on social welfare and religious discipline. Pastors, teachers, deacons and elders were appointed to improve educational and pastoral care, and in this respect Bucer's reformation was markedly different from what had been established in Wittenberg. Luther's doctrine of the Two Kingdoms had advocated the separateness of Church and state, while Bucer's Church Orders in Strasburg promoted the role of the Church in social and political affairs. Ultimately, the council in Strasburg reigned-in Bucer's programme of social reform, refusing his wish to place discipline in the hands of the Church elders.

In 1536 Bucer's ongoing efforts to bring about unity between Protestant groups appeared to succeed when the south German cities came to an agreement with the Lutherans known as the Wittenberg Concord. With the collapse of Zwinglianism in Switzerland it was vital for the political and economic security of the southern German cities that they align themselves with Lutheran towns. Bucer and Melanchthon were pivotal in the negotiations which appeared, initially, to settle the dispute over the Lord's Supper. Yet unity was relatively short-lived as the Swiss believed that Bucer had given too much ground to Luther on the real presence of Christ in the Eucharist. Indeed, Bucer himself disavowed the agreement at a later stage. In Strasburg, Bucer still operated a policy of religious toleration even towards minority groups such as the Anabaptists, who were ruthlessly persecuted elsewhere.

What was Bucer's significance?

- After Luther and Melanchthon, Bucer was the most important German reformer of the sixteenth century.
- Bucer's interpretation of the Eucharist and his programme of social welfare reform set him apart from Luther.
- Bucer always seemed willing to compromise doctrine in order to establish unity.
- Bucer was not only a key figure in trying to establish a middle ground amongst Protestants, but also central to efforts at reconciliation between Catholics and Protestants at Regensburg in 1541.
- Bucer rejected the Augsburg Interim in 1548 on the grounds that it would turn back the reformation in Strasburg. Under pressure from imperial armies, Bucer found his position in Strasburg untenable, and, in 1548, he travelled to England at the invitation of Thomas Cranmer, Archbishop of Canterbury. He subsequently had a profound influence on the direction of the English Reformation under Edward VI.

HULDRYCH ZWINGLI

KEY ISSUES

Luther's view of Zwingli is important for **Key Issue 3** (see page iv).

Outside Germany, the Reformation spread and diversified. Huldrych Zwingli (1484–1531) had already emerged as one of the leading humanists within the Swiss Confederation when he arrived in Zurich in 1519 to become priest of that city.

The beliefs of Zwingli

Zwingli's sermons in those early years as people's priest continued to reflect his humanist past.

- Erasmian criticisms of the superstitious nature of Catholicism were preached.
- Above all else, direct contact with the Bible and the word of God was emphasised.
- However, between 1520 and 1522, Zwingli adopted the doctrines of justification by faith alone and *sola scriptura* (scriptural authority), thereby aligning himself closely with Luther.

Zwingli later stressed that any similarities were a coincidence, and it is debatable just how greatly Zwingli was influenced by the German reformer.

Zwingli the reformer

Zwingli's status and standing as a reformer grew in 1522 when he openly defended a case of fast-breaking during Lent, delivering a sermon entitled *On Choice and Liberty in Food*. Moreover, by the end of 1522 he had broken the vows of clerical celibacy. Nothing in these actions or opinions varies greatly from Luther, indeed the similarities are striking. Within Zurich, a split was beginning to become apparent on the city council and among the populace. The split was between:

- those in favour of reform who wanted a quicker pace of change.
- the traditional Catholics who had already seen enough reform for their liking.

In January 1523, a disputation was called by the Zurich city council which intended to restore order by deciding upon the legitimacy of Zwingli's preaching. The local bishop, the Bishop of Constance, refused to attend such a lay gathering. Zwingli, however, prepared his **Sixty-Seven Theses** for the disputation. Although his theses were largely ignored, the Council did call for preaching in the city to be based on the word of God. The principle of evangelical preaching based on the Gospel had been endorsed by a secular power – that is, the Zurich city council.

The Reformation in Zurich

Zwingli now had a more favourable environment in which to operate and introduce further reform. On 15 June 1524, all images were removed from churches in the city, and in December the monasteries of the city were secularised. Finally, in June 1525, the Mass was abolished and replaced by a fully reformed **Lord's Supper**. The Reformation in Zurich had moved swiftly, but across the rest of the Swiss Confederation there was initially less enthusiasm. The five states of central Switzerland reaffirmed their commitment to Catholicism. Yet in Berne, the largest and most powerful state, there was a more favourable reaction. The Mass was abolished there in 1528, while one year later Basle, greatly influenced by the reformer **Johannes Oecolampadius**, also threw in its lot with the Reformation. By 1529 only one-third of the Swiss population lived in Catholic states.

Zwingli wished to see the spread of the Reformation, and he was willing to endorse military force to do so if necessary. Two camps were clearly emerging within the Swiss Confederation as it drifted towards civil war. The Catholic states backed by Habsburg aid were potentially formidable. However, both sides were unenthusiastic about the prospect of a bloody civil conflict over religion.

- **First Kappel War**, 1529. This was demonstrated by the bloodless First Kappel War in which neither army was willing to encroach upon enemy territory.
- **Second Kappel War**, 1531. The Second Kappel War of 1531 was more conclusive. Divisions within the Reformist side existed between Zurich, which wished to use direct military action, and Berne, which favoured an economic blockade of the five central states. These divisions were made worse by the inability of Luther and Zwingli to agree on the degree of real presence in the Eucharist. Therefore the Reformers were deprived of Schmalkaldic assistance in their fight against the Catholic states. In October 1531, Zwingli's forces were routed at the Battle of Kappel and Zwingli was among those killed.

KEY EVENTS

The Kappel Wars were conflicts deriving from the religious split in Zurich in 1524–5. Five of the thirteen Swiss states embraced the Reformation and fought to maintain the true word of God. The wars accounted for Zwingli in 1531 before a peace settlement was reached in November 1531, which enabled the rulers of each state to decide the religion.

The peace treaties that followed described Catholicism as the true, undoubted faith and conversion to Protestantism was forbidden. However, no attempt was made to return Zurich and Berne to the Catholic fold and Zwinglianism lived on in the north of Switzerland and smaller pockets in the south before the arrival of Calvinism in the 1540s lessened its significance.

A COMPARISON OF ZWINGLI AND LUTHER

There are a number of similarities and differences between the two reformers:

Academic ability: Unquestionably, these two reformers differ little in this regard. Both demonstrated outstanding academic ability and both entered a life in the clergy.

Influences: Zwingli was greatly influenced by humanist professors such as Thomas Wittenbach at the University of Basle and, like Luther, he devoted himself to learning Greek and translating scripture. Moreover, both were influenced by Erasmus, with Zwingli first reading his works in 1516 by which time Luther was well acquainted with them and on the verge, albeit unknowingly, of sparking off the German Reformation.

Impact: Here lies the first major and very obvious difference. Despite being only a year older, Luther made his impact earlier and more explosively than Zwingli. While the message of the two reformers in terms of Church reform was very similar, in some respects, Zwingli was overshadowed by the early impact Luther had made. For example, by 1521 Luther had been condemned by both Emperor and Pope and Lutheranism was evolving as a powerful force within the towns. In 1521, Zwingli had only just begun to be noticed as a public reformist figure in Zurich, and was just coming to terms with justification by faith alone and *sola scriptura*.

Environment: The very environment in which Luther was reforming was, as we have seen, most helpful in developing and spreading his message. Zwingli, on the other hand, could not call on the culturally advanced and semi-literate cities to help his ideas to evolve. The Swiss message was therefore always going to be slow to develop and spread. Another problem for Zwingli was that following so closely in the footsteps of Luther was also likely to dilute the appeal of Zwinglianism. However, Zwingli's influence did slowly spread into south Germany, to cities such as Strasburg and Memmingen. Yet any chance of expansion here was limited because, in turning to the ideas of the Swiss, Zwingli may have isolated these cities politically and economically from the Holy Roman Empire. Therefore, while both men acted as figureheads for reform, it was inevitable that Luther would front the larger and more successful movement.

Similarities of doctrine: The similarities between the two men should perhaps have allowed for a unification of the two strands of Protestantism. Doctrinally they agreed on the path to salvation, while both stressed the duty of the subject to obey his lord. Luther's political influence in Wittenberg may have been greater, but the endorsement of the city council in Zurich was crucial to Zwingli's success.

Doctrinal differences: One issue in particular divided Luther and Zwingli, preventing a united Protestant front. Over the sacrament of the Eucharist and in particular the words of Christ, ***Hoc est corpus meum***, no agreement could be found. Luther's position, as we have already seen, was relatively conservative, in that he denied the element of sacrifice in the Catholic sacrament and the notion of a miracle taking place, but he did stress that the body of Christ was physically present in the Eucharist. For Zwingli, the sacrament was purely symbolic, and the real presence was denied. By 1529, it became clear that a solution was required and, to this end, Philip of Hesse invited both Zwingli and Luther to Marburg in order to debate the issue. Already, Luther had outlined his position personally in print to Zwingli in an aggressive work entitled *Confession on Christ's Supper* (1528). Agreement was impossible and the chance for unity lost. The south German cities returned to the Lutheran fold through the Four Cities Confession of 1530 and then later with the Wittenberg Concord of 1536.

CONCLUSION

Ultimately, one should not view Zwingli as a radical. Luther regarded him as such because of **personal rivalry**, his denial of the real presence and his endorsement of military force to further the word of God, the latter being a position which Luther himself would have adopted by 1537. Zwingli did manage to oversee a disciplined and bloodless reformation in Zurich, which was consolidated by Heinrich Bullinger. Moreover, the close co-operation between Church and State, which Zwingli had encouraged, was later to be replicated by Calvin in Geneva.

WHAT WAS THE SIGNIFCANCE OF THE ANABAPTISTS?

What were the ideas of the Anabaptists?
Essentially, the Anabaptists were the real radicals of the early Reformation in Europe. They represented a small and extremely diverse group that had become discontented with the moderate nature of mainstream reform. Luther and Zwingli had initiated Church reform, but some believed that they had failed to see it through to its natural end.

- For the Anabaptists, Luther had been too conservative and had bowed to authority on too many occasions, leaving a church that was little better than before.
- Allegiance to Rome had been shattered but, according to the Anabaptists, further reform was required through which certainty of faith and commitment to a Christian lifestyle could be assured.
- Zwingli called this group Anabaptists (from 'anti-Baptists') as a consequence of their rejection of infant baptism. **Anabaptists** were re-baptisers, in that they believed in adult baptism, because only with maturity and experience could one understand the significance of this sacrament.
- The Anabaptist movement was a wide-ranging one and tended to attract fanatical **demagogues** who played upon the Anabaptists' belief that visions and inner voices constituted direct communication with God.

KEY TERMS

Anabaptists It should be pointed out that anabaptists was a term used by their opponents. They did not see themselves as re-baptisers.

Demagogue A leader of the people who attracts support through oratory.

Instances of violence and immorality in south Germany in 1525, north Germany in 1534, as well as in the Swiss cantons and the Netherlands tarnished Anabaptism with an extremist and dangerous brush. This view was unfair as the violence and immorality were practised by a small minority. Anabaptism began as a spiritual, intellectual and pacifistic movement, which was hijacked by extremist figureheads. Despite ferocious persecution, Anabaptism continued to flourish in the Netherlands and, later, in America.

KEY ISSUES

Müntzer, and Luther's view of him, is important for **Key Issue 3** (see page iv).

Thomas Müntzer (1489–1525)

Trained as a priest, Müntzer was a conventional supporter of Luther in Saxony, before becoming more radical in his defence of the Zwickau Prophets (see page 47) in 1521. In July 1524, he preached a sermon in which he revealed his belief in direct communication with God through dreams and visions. Apparently he was one of the 'godly,' and now it was time to turn on the ungodly with force. Müntzer's followers were generally from the lower classes of society; attracted by his message of equality and redistribution of wealth. In 1524, he moved to Mühlhausen, which was at the centre of the Peasants' Revolt. In alliance with Heinrich Pfeiffer, the peasants had overthrown the city council and were beginning to restore lands to the people through force. Yet in May 1525 the revolt was abruptly stopped when the peasant armies were routed outside Frankenhausen. Müntzer was captured, tortured and killed.

The North German and Dutch Anabaptists

The most important Anabaptist leader was Melchior Hoffmann (d. 1543), who was based in Emden in East Friesland. Hoffmann and his followers re-baptised hundreds of people in the Netherlands. His ideas spread to north German towns such as Münster and Cologne. Hoffmann preached an **apocalyptic message**:

- He claimed that he was the prophet **Elijah** and that the world would end in 1533.
- He also argued that the ungodly needed to be cleansed before the Second Coming of Christ.
- However, he did not suggest the use of force in purifying the community, stating rather conservatively that only **magistrates** should use the sword.
- Strasburg was to be the gathering point for the 'godly,' where the end of the world would be awaited.

Yet the Last Days did not come, and when a self-professed prophet outlives judgement day, his followers tend to lose faith. Hoffman died in prison in 1543. However, his apprentices were to prove more radical.

Münster

Many of Hoffmann's supporters did maintain a belief in Anabaptism, which was continued in the Westphalian town of Münster in 1533. Hundreds were attracted to northwest Germany from the Netherlands, including Jan van Leiden, a Dutch tailor. Under the guidance of the reformer Bernard Rothmann, Münster began to move towards Anabaptism. Over 1400 people in Münster were re-baptised. In February 1533, the Anabaptists took power in the town of Münster with their leader Jan Mathijs being voted into power. However, the prince bishop of Münster laid siege to the city in February 1534, a siege that lasted 16 months. In many ways this military threat radicalised the stance of those within the city walls. All those who did not want to join the Anabaptists were encouraged to leave the city, while all private property was abolished and

KEY TERMS

Apocalyptic message This is a message that predicts that the end of the world is coming soon.

KEY PEOPLE

The prophet **Elijah** is an important figure in the Old Testament part of the Bible. Elijah argued for the worship of God rather than pagan gods.

KEY TERMS

Magistrates are those who made up the ruling oligarchy of sixteenth-century towns.

historical records destroyed. So convinced was the Anabaptist leader, Jan Matthijs, that the second coming was near and that the kingdom of God was to be founded in Münster that he charged headlong into the besieging troops, and was killed.

Jan van Leiden

His successor was Jan van Leiden, who introduced an Old Testament kingship based on **polygamy** and dictatorial rule. King Jan was the self-proclaimed new King David in the New Jerusalem of Münster. He took 16 wives and the immorality and harsh rule that followed did much to harm the reputation of Anabaptism. With food running low and morale falling daily, the city was eventually betrayed from within on 25 June 1535. Troops entered the city and brutally tortured and killed the inhabitants. Jan van Leiden was paraded around northern Germany before being killed in January 1536 in the market place of Münster, while others were beheaded before being exhibited in iron cages that hung from the city church as an example to others of what became of such radicals. Anabaptism never really recovered from the blow, and the movement split into several factions. The most successful of these factions were the pacifist followers of **Menno Simons** in the Netherlands.

KEY TERMS

Polygamy is the practice of having more than one wife at a time.

KEY PEOPLE

Menno Simons (1496–1561) endured the survival of a more moderate brand of Anabaptism during a period (1536–61) of severe persecution. Through his missionary work in Germany and Netherlands, he spread the doctrine of adult baptism and the rejection of clerical oaths. By 1572, the Mennonites had been granted toleration in the Netherlands and part of Germany.

ACTIVITY

Enquiries
Luther and Zwingli

(a) **Study Sources D and E**

Compare these Sources as evidence for the meeting between Luther and Zwingli at Marburg in 1529.

(b) **Study all the Sources**

How far do these Sources support the interpretation that Luther was intolerant as a religious leader?

Source A: The leading Catholic humanist blames Luther in particular for the arguments about religion that Luther had with other religious reformers.

I deplore the constant in-fighting between religious leaders. Apart from the Zwickau Prophets and the Anabaptists, just look at the spiteful pamphlets written by Luther and Zwingli against each other. I have always condemned the venom of such religious leaders, and their followers encourage them. They should have set an example of godly and patient conduct which would have made God's truth widely acceptable. Did Luther not realise how foolish he looked? This is the movement's leader!

Erasmus, letter to Martin Bucer,
the leading religious reformer in Strasburg, 1527

Source B: An eye witness report of opening statements at a meeting between Luther and other leading reformers to resolve religious disputes between Protestants. The meeting was organised by Count Philip of Hesse.

The Chancellor of Hesse: My gracious Prince, Philip of Hesse, has called you to this meeting in order to settle the quarrel about the Lord's Supper. Much depends on it. My Prince wishes that everybody should seek God's honour, not his own advantage, in a spirit of brotherly friendship.

Luther: Illustrious Prince! I do not doubt that this meeting has been planned with good intentions. I agreed to come when Philip made preparations for it. I felt that I had to obey the wishes of this most excellent ruler. But I do not want to change my view, which is as firm as a rock.

Report of the Colloquy of Marburg, October 1529

Source C: A well informed report of the argument between Luther and other reformers at the Marburg Colloquy.

Zwingli: You won't give ground because you are prejudiced and have already made up your mind. You won't yield until somebody quotes a passage in the Bible. We agree on the most important points and I beg you in Christ's name not to call somebody a heretic because of other differences. We both agree that it is impossible for God to order us to eat Christ's flesh at the Lord's Supper in a physical sense. Don't be offended by what I say. I disagree with you in a friendly manner.

Luther: The only way to settle the argument between us is for you to keep God's word and agree with me.

Report of the Colloquy of Marburg, October 1529

Source D: A letter from Luther to his wife, Katherine von Bora, straight after the Colloquy of Marburg.

Our friendly conference at Marburg is now at an end and we are in perfect union in all points except that our opponents insist that there is simply bread and wine in the Lord's Supper, and that Christ is in it in a spiritual sense. Today Philip of Hesse did his best to make us united, hoping that even though we disagreed we should hold to each other as brothers and members of Christ. He worked hard for it, but we would not call them brothers or members of Christ, although we wish them well and desire to remain at peace.

Luther, letter to Katharine von Bora, November 1529

Source E: A letter from Zwingli to one of his supporters immediately after the Colloquy of Marburg.

Three times we threw at Luther the fact that he had at other times given a different exposition from the one he was now insisting on of those ridiculous ideas of his… but the dear man had nothing to say in reply. He conceded that the body of Christ is finite. He conceded that the Eucharist may be called a sign of the body of Christ. These are examples of his countless inconsistencies, absurdities and follies; but we refuted him so successfully that Philip of Hesse has now come down on our side. The truth prevailed so manifestly that if ever a man was beaten in this world, it was Luther.

Zwingli, letter to a supporter, November 1529

What were Luther's views on other Protestants?

SUMMARY

What had the Lutheran Reformation achieved?

The Reformation is difficult to gauge simply in terms of successes and failures. After all, Luther himself had not set out to create a new faith, and his excommunication in 1520 was hardly in line with his original intentions. That said, the Lutheran Reformation made a huge impact in the 1520s on the social, cultural and political landscape of Germany and the whole of Europe.

- At the start of the sixteenth century there had only been one faith in the Holy Roman Empire and by 1555 there were two.
- The doctrine and practices of the late medieval Catholic Church vanished in Protestant states as indulgences, purgatory and the cult of saints became irrelevant.
- The sermon replaced the Mass as the central focus of worship in the Protestant world and the Bible emerged as the supreme authority in doctrinal matters. That the Bible was read in the vernacular highlights the impact of the Reformation on language.
- Church interiors changed, as ornate decoration was spurned in favour of 'Godly' simplicity. The visual focus of the Church now became the pulpit from where the sermon would be delivered.
- The clerical hierarchy was destroyed by the priesthood of all believers and clergymen became ordinary citizens. Clerical marriage could now take place and some women even preached the Gospel publicly, enhancing their status in the process.
- By the end of the sixteenth century seven out of every ten people in the Holy Roman Empire were officially Lutheran. Large numbers of schools were established in Protestant areas as reformers stressed the need for basic educational standards to be upheld.
- Lutheranism paved the way for other Protestant churches and perhaps hastened the Catholic Church into reforming its doctrine and organisation.

That said, the early enthusiasm for Lutheranism did not last and it should be noted that the long term impact of the movement was largely confined to Germany and Scandinavia.

- By the 1530s it was clear that the future of Lutheranism lay in the hands of the princes. The Peasants' Revolt of 1525 had shown that the ordinary people could not be trusted to interpret the scriptures for themselves. Catechisms and primers were published to educate the masses, and the clergy were instructed to guide the ordinary people in their spiritual lives. As a result the liberating message of Luther which had resounded throughout the 1520s was somewhat lost in later years.
- Lutheranism became, for some princes, a vehicle for political power or material wealth as can be seen through the wars of the 1540s and 50s between 'Protestant' states led by their princes and the Holy Roman Emperor Charles V.
- Initial hopes that the role of women in society might advance were also quickly dashed in the 1530s as patriarchal, traditional values were reimposed.
- Lutheran visitations in the 1530s revealed a populace which still clung to the old ways. The process of conversion was going to be a long one and Luther was somewhat disappointed with the conduct of his clergy and the ignorance of the people. The initial enthusiasm and optimism of the 1520s died out when Luther began to try to implement a permanent framework for reform.
- The historian Gerald Strauss has shown that in many rural areas old superstitious practices continued to exist and that Lutheran doctrine appeared to have made little impact.

Therefore, one could argue that Lutheranism never quite lived up to the excitement that it generated in the 1520s. However, there remains little doubt that the effect of the Lutheran Reformation on the political identity of the Holy Roman Empire combined with the religious shockwaves created by Luther's movement made an indelible impact on the history of Early Modern Europe.

BIBLIOGRAPHY

T.A. Brady. H.A. Oberman and J.D. Tracy (eds), *Handbook of European History 1400–1600*, Eerdmans Publishing, 1995

S. Brigden, *London and the Reformation*, Oxford, 1989

Euan Cameron, *The European Reformation*, Clarendon Press, 1991

G.R. Elton, *Reformation Europe 1517–1559*, Blackwell, 1963

J. Lotherington, *Years of Renewal*, Hodder, 1998

A.D.M. Pettegree, *The Reformation in the Parishes*, Cambridge, 1990

A.D.M. Pettegree, *The Early Reformation in Europe*, Cambridge, 1992

A.D.M. Pettegree, *The Reformation World*, Routledge, 2000

K. Randall, *Luther and the German Reformation*, Hodder, 1988

Jasper Ridley, *John Knox*, Oxford, 1968

Exam Café
Relax, refresh, result!

Relax and prepare

Student tips!

Jack

I got good marks for History at GCSE so thought I would adapt to the AS level easily but it was much harder than I expected as you have to find out a lot more stuff for yourself and read around the subject rather than just doing what the teacher says. It took a bit of getting used to but now I'm doing A2 it's my favourite subject!

Cassie

I would have found it really helpful to have had a copy of the specification I was following at the very start. I was well into the course before I realised that the different units of the exam were looking for different things so I treated the period study unit in the same way as the enquiries unit at the start until I realised that the emphasis in the enquiries units is on analysing sources rather than just writing about your knowledge of the period.

Sally

I always make revision notes. The most important part of the revision notes is to come up with questions to ask of the information in the sources. This means that I am thinking about the information all of the time rather than simply writing all the points down.

Asima

In my mock exams I made the mistake of not taking enough time to think about my answers and plan them before I started writing – luckily my teacher pointed this out to me and I spent lots of my revision time for the actual exams practising planning answers to practise questions. It really paid off!

Oliver

I found it helpful to carry out practice source exercises as I covered the content of the enquiries paper. This way I felt that I was learning the skills necessary for success as well as learning the detail of the key events. I found out that the most important thing in the enquiries paper was learning how to answer the questions and developing the techniques required to get a top grade.

Getting Started

Creating an interrogation dossier

The historian is like a detective in that it is his or her job to enquire into what has happened. The only way that this can be done is by using evidence. However, like a detective, the historian has to ask questions of the evidence in order to find out how reliable and useful it is. Remember that a source that is not reliable may still be useful.

Your first task is to build up a bank of questions that you can use when evaluating sources. To set up your interrogation dossier you need to divide a page of A4 into two or use a double page in an exercise book.

The first set of questions that you should draw up should be under the following headings:

a. **Content/context/situation**: These will be questions that relate to what the source shows or says, the background to the production of the source and the position or situation of the author of the source when the source was produced.

    Here are a few questions to get you started:
    *   *When was the source produced?*
    *   *Was there censorship at the time?*
    *   *Was the author in a position to know?*

    Now it is your turn to come up with as many questions as you can.

b. **Purpose/nature**: These will be questions that relate to reasons why the source was produced and its form; whether it is a painting, cartoon or an extract from a diary, letter, newspaper and so forth.

    Here are a few questions to start you off:
    *   *Is the source propaganda?*
    *   *Does the author attempt to distort the evidence?*
    *   *Is the extract drawn as a piece of satire?*

The more questions that you can come up with, the better will be your evaluation of the sources. You may wish to compare the questions that you have come up with to the person next to you in class.

Once you have drawn up your interrogation dossier, you should keep it in a safe place and refer to it whenever you are evaluating evidence.

Revision Checklist

Key Issue 1 What were Luther's main ideas and how and to whom did they spread?

- The cause and impact of Luther's Ninety-Five Theses
- The development of Luther's ideas as expressed in *On the Babylonish Captivity of the Church* and *An Appeal to the Christian Nobility of the German Nation*
- Luther's theology: *sola fide, sola scriptura* and the priesthood of all believers
- The appeal of Luther's ideas to the German people
- The role of the printing press in spreading Luther's ideas.

Key Issue 2 How did the authorities react to Luther from 1517 to 1521?

- The Catholic reaction to Luther
- Luther's meeting with Cajetan at Augsburg in 1518
- Luther's meeting with Eck at Leipzig in 1519
- The Bull *Exsurge Domine* 1520
- The Diet of Worms 1521
- The support of Frederick the Wise 1517–25.

Key Issue 3 What was the impact of Lutheranism in Germany from 1517 to 1530?

- The development and spread of Lutheranism in the cities
- The reaction of the princes to Luther's ideas
- The extent to which Lutheranism caused the Peasants' Revolt of 1525
- Problems facing Charles V in dealing with Lutheranism
- The Diet of Speyer 1526
- The Diet of Speyer 1529
- Divisions within Protestantism: Marburg Colloquy 1529
- The Diet of Augsburg and the Confession of Augsburg 1530
- Radical Reformation: Zwingli and the Anabaptists.

Key Issue 4 Why did Lutheranism survive in Germany between 1530 and 1555?

- Princely Support

- Schmalkaldic League and the leadership of Philip of Hesse

- Ongoing problems of Charles V

- Battle of Muhlberg 1547

- Augsburg Interim 1548

- Princely Revolt 1552

- Religious Peace of Augsburg 1555.

Key Ideas/Questions

Here are some important ideas to think about while you are revising:

- To what extent did Luther pose a serious challenge to the Church in 1517?

- How important was Luther to the success of the Reformation in Germany?

- What was the reaction of the Catholic Church to Luther in the period 1520–5?

- How/why did Lutheranism become a popular movement in the period 1520–5?

- Why does 1525 mark a turning point in the Reformation in Germany?

- How was the Lutheran movement consolidated after 1525?

- Why was Charles V unable to deal effectively with Luther 1519–55?

- How important were the princes in supporting Lutheranism in the period 1530–55?

Get the result!

Remember that on the Historical Enquiries Paper, you will be faced with two questions:

The (a) question will always ask you to compare two sources. It is worth 30 marks and you should spend roughly 30 minutes on this question.

That leaves you 60 minutes to deal with the (b) question which requires you to use all the sources and your own knowledge and is worth 70 marks.

(a) Questions

Examiner's tips

- You have roughly 30 minutes for this answer. Make sure you spend 5-10 minutes planning. Once you know the significant areas of agreement and disagreement it will not take long to actually write the answer.

- You do not need to overcomplicate things! Keep your answer clear and focused. The key to a top mark is thinking about why the sources differ/agree, not just how they differ/agree.

- Make a point by point comparison. That means that you have to deal with the sources together, not separately, in order to make a proper comparison.

- Use short quotations to reinforce your points but use your own words to explain the points of comparison.

- Always look to compare as underline evidence for something.

- Remember that you don't need to use any own knowledge explicitly in this question. However you will need to know the context of both sources in order to evaluate them effectively. That means thinking about the situation and purpose of the author as well as their audience. Also look at the date as this will give you an idea of what is happening at the time and may explain the content and tone of the source.

Structuring your answer to (a) questions:

- The first two paragraphs are comprehension-style accounts of the similarities and differences between the two sources. But make sure that you stick to the focus of the question.

- The third paragraph examines provenance – <u>why</u> the sources agree/disagree

- Finally come to a conclusion.

- Right, let's have a look at a candidate's answer to an (a) question:

The Catholic Reaction to Luther

(a) Study Sources A and B

Compare these Sources as evidence for the reactions of the papacy to Luther's message.

Source A

Martin Luther, at the suggestion of the Devil, has said evil about us and the papacy, in preaching and cursing. This resembles heresy and deserves severe punishment. Because of your devotion and obedience to the papacy, it should not be tolerated. We should root up this weed from God's field in case it takes root among simple people.

Pope Leo X, letter to Duke George of Saxony, October 1518

Source B

Cajetan stated that he did not wish to argue with me, but to settle the matter peacefully and in a fatherly fashion. He said that the Pope demanded that I should do three things. First, I should come to my senses and withdraw my errors, secondly promise not to repeat them in the future, and thirdly I should not do anything to disturb the Church. I immediately asked to be told how I had been wrong because I was not conscious of any errors. I declared that I was not conscious of having said anything contrary to the Bible, the Church Fathers or papal announcements. All that I said seems to me entirely sensible, true and Catholic. Nevertheless, since I am a man who can make a mistake, I would submit to the judgement of the Church and to all who were better informed than me.

Luther's publication, *Proceedings at Augsburg*, November 1518

Examiner says:

The candidate makes a good start in using short quotations from the sources and in analysing the sources together and not separately.

Asima's Answer

Both Sources A and B agree that the papacy disagreed with Luther's teachings and saw them as heretical. In Source A the Pope writes that Luther's ideas resemble heresy whilst in Source B the Pope told Luther to withdraw his errors. Therefore both Sources A and B see the Papacy taking quite a hard line on Luther. Both Sources also agree that the Papacy viewed Luther's teachings as damaging and dangerous. In Source A Leo X states that action must be taken against Luther before his ideas take root among simple people. This is reinforced in Source B when Luther writes that the Pope warned him not to disturb the Church. It is clear that the Papacy feared that Luther's teachings might become popular and undermine the Catholic faith.

The Sources differ in their provenance and purpose. Source A was written by the Pope Leo X himself and therefore we would expect his views on Luther to be harsh. It is no surprise that he describes Luther as a weed from God's field that needs to be uprooted. Source B on the other hand is an account of Luther's meeting with Cajetan by Luther himself. It suggests a slightly less aggressive approach from the Catholic authorities, especially from Cajetan himself who wanted to settle the matter peacefully and in a fatherly fashion. The difference in tone might be explained by the purpose of the two authors. In Source A the Pope was writing to Duke George of Saxony, a fiercely Catholic prince in order to convince him of the need to act against Luther. Luther on the other hand was merely recording what happened at his meeting with Cajetan at Augsburg whilst still trying to convince the authorities of his loyalty to Catholicism. In Source B Luther writes I would submit to the judgement of the Church which clearly suggests that he is no revolutionary whilst in Source A the Pope has told Duke George that Luther should not be tolerated.

Examiner's comments

The candidate continues an excelle[nt] answer by examinin[g] the provenance of both sources and using this to explain differences betwee[n] them.

Therefore the sources both agree that the papacy saw Luther's teachings as false but disagree on how the Pope suggested Luther should be dealt with. In Source A the Pope suggests very harsh treatment of Luther but Luther himself in Source B says that the Pope would treat him more leniantly.

Examiner's comments

The end of the answer is a little short but importantly the candidate does come to a conclusion which is directly related to the question.

Examiner's tips

You have left yourself 1 hour to complete the (b) question. Again make sure you spend 10 minutes planning your answer and thinking about which sources agree/disagree with the statement and why that might be the case. (Tips on how to write a plan are provided below.)

- Highlight the focus of the question from the start and shape your argument around it.

- Try to group the sources around the focus of the question, do not just deal with the sources in the order that they appear on the sheet.

- Be prepared to evaluate the provenance and reliability of source material as you go along.

- Develop a sense of argument or discussion rather than just a survey.

- Utilise short quotations from the sources to reinforce your point but always explain that point in your own words.

- Integrate your own knowledge as you go along to bring in issues or events that are not included in the sources – make it specific and relevant to your argument and do not write a paragraph which is solely own knowledge based. You don't need much own knowledge to gain credit from the examiner. Many candidates waste time by including knowledge which is not relevant to the question. Keep it short, sharp and relevant.

- Try to form a balanced judgement on the question in light of the sources.

Writing a plan

- Draw up a table of two columns. One column should be for sources which agree with the question and one should be for sources which disagree.

- Fit each source to a column. Don't worry if you think that one source might fit both columns, in fact you will probably find that several of the sources appear in both columns. You must include every source.

- Now get a highlighter out and highlight one or two key quotations from each source to show how it fits your argument. Use a different colour to highlight 'agrees' and 'disagrees'.

- Next, add points of evaluation to your plan. Look carefully at each author and date. Think about the provenance of each source. Ask yourself <u>why</u> the author was writing, <u>who</u> they were writing for and <u>whether</u> they were in a position to know about the topic. Look at the language and the perspective of the author – how does this relate to the content?

- Finally add some relevant own knowledge to your plan. This means information which can't be found in the sources. Try to integrate that own knowledge into your argument. Don't just lump it all into one paragraph.

- Now you are ready to write your answer out properly in continuous prose!

Structuring your answer

- Write a short introduction to your answer where you set out your argument.

- Use the first couple of paragraphs to discuss the sources which agree with your argument – don't forget to evaluate as you go along and include your own knowledge.

- Then use the next couple of paragraphs to discuss the sources which disagree, again evaluate as you go along and use your own knowledge where relevant.

- Finally write a concluding paragraph where you weigh up the evidence and come to a conclusion – remember to make a short and sharp judgement on the question.

- Right let's have a look at a candidates answer to a (b) question.

Luther's opposition to indulgences

(b) Study all the Sources

Use your own knowledge to assess how far the sources support the interpretation that Luther's opposition to indulgences was the main reason why he attracted religious support.

Source A: Martin Luther writes to an important church official, who was also a secular ruler to persuade him to suppress the indulgences offered by Tetzel in his lands.

An indulgence from Pope Leo is sold under the protection of your illustrious name for the building of St Peter's at Rome. I am greatly concerned at the false ideas the common people have. They believe their salvation is certain as soon as they buy this indulgence. How is it possible that indulgence sellers give security to the people through such false promises? A new church may be needed to keep safe the bones of St Peter, but I earnestly request you to cancel your permission to the indulgence sellers and order them to preach differently. Otherwise your reputation might suffer.

> Martin Luther, letter to Albert, Elector and
> Archbishop of Mainz, 31 October 1517

Source B: A reformer and early supporter of Luther describes the popularity of the indulgences preached by Johann Tetzel in 1517.

Johann Tetzel, a preacher of indulgences in Germany, raised enormous amounts of money which was then sent to Rome. His indulgences were so highly prized that, when he entered a town, the papal authorisation for the indulgence was carried on gold cloth. All the priests, monks, members of the town council, men, women and children met him in a solemn procession. All the bells were rung and all the organs played. Even God himself could not have been welcomed and entertained with more honour. We Germans are fools to be robbed in this way.

> Friedrich Myconius, an account written in 1519

Source C: A German Catholic humanist writes a balanced account of the controversy over indulgences to a leading Swiss reformer.

There is much in Luther that should be praised and defended. But there is also much that seems offensive. He thinks that the Pope does not have universal authority by the will of God. I cannot emphasise enough how much this claim displeases me. It contradicts the teaching of the Church. Luther criticises popes and almost spits on them as if they are irrelevant, and does so without law or reason. I have my own thoughts about indulgences but do not want to express them; I have no desire to get into trouble. People have debated indulgences for years and we need a decision by a Church Council to settle this, but reform of many other abuses that trouble the church is more urgent. Luther has tried boldly but with little success to resolve the problem of indulgences, even though his many little pamphlets seem to be everywhere.

Ulrich Zasius, letter to Zwingli, 1519

Source D: The leading humanist complains about the condition of the Church.

Alas! Christianity has sunk so low that few men even know what it means to pray to God. As head of the Church the Pope deserves honour. But he overstretched his authority. Monks and commissioners sold indulgences – acceptable within limits – but they did it everywhere just to get rich. Bishops need to root out the corruptions among the clergy; and monasteries are in an even worse state.

Erasmus, letter to Botzheim, another humanist, August 1529

Source E: Luther writes about the importance of scripture.

If we quote the Bible to the Church authorities, they object that only the Pope can interpret it. It is a wicked fable that only the Pope can interpret the Bible. The Church authorities have seized this authority for themselves. Spiritual authority was not given only to the Pope but to the whole community. If we believe in the priesthood of all believers, should we not have the power to examine and decide what is right or wrong in religious matters? The Bible should make us free and bold, and the spirit of freedom should not be chased away by the inventions of the Pope.

Martin Luther, *An Appeal to the Christian Nobility of the German Nation*, 1520

Cassie's Answer

Luther's opposition to indulgences in 1517 was an important reason for his popularity and it brought him publicity and notoriety and served to place him in direct conflict with the Catholic Church. However, it is debatable whether it was the main reason he attracted support.

As Source A reveals, Luther believed the sale of indulgences to be corrupt and he is critical of German money being used to build a new basilica in Rome – building of St Peters. In reality the money raised was being used by the recipient of Luther's letter to pay off debts incurred in bribing his way to becoming the Archbishop of Mainz. The idea of financial corruption is reinforced in Source B when Myconius writes that the German people are being robbed by Rome. Even the moderate Erasmus agrees in D that indulgences were sold everywhere so that monks and commissioners could get rich. Luther's criticism of indulgences was based on the idea that salvation could not be purchased and this is seen in Source A when he writes about the false promises of indulgence sellers. Indulgences were popular as Myconius outlines when he states in B that they were highly prized and that all the people of the town came out to greet Tetzel. Therefore Luther's revelations about the greed and corruption of Rome combined with his increasing belief that salvation could not be attained so easily was always likely to gain him notoriety and in certain parts of Germany popularity. The 95 theses were soon translated into German and spread through various cities. As Myconius stresses the German nature of the indulgences controversy was crucial as there was an increasing feeling that honest Germans were being exploited by Rome. Clearly the indulgences controversy was the trigger for Luther's criticism of the Catholic Church and the popular Reformation even if he did not intend for this to be the case. Indeed in Source A Luther seems concerned about the reputation of the Archbishop of Mainz whom he labels illustrious and asks him to alter the message of his preachers so that indulgences alone are not seen as the means of salvation. It must be remembered that Luther was an Augustinian monk and a member of the Church – he himself would state later that he had not intended for his ideas to spread widely or rapidly.

Examiner's comments

This is a good paragraph. It conveys a sense of argument, reinforces points with short quotations and addresses the provenance of the sources. To reach the top level Cassie needs to analyse the sources and integrate this into her answer.

Sources C, D and E take different lines on Luther and his opposition to indulgences. Source C agrees with A and B in seeing indulgences as a problem but not to the same extent as Luther. Zasius finds Luther offensive and takes a less radical stance on the Papacy. He makes an important point that the debate on indulgences was nothing new which must then put Myconius's national sentiment in an even more important light. The anticlericalism and disillusionment with the Catholic Church in Saxony meant that Luther's call for indulgence sales to stop met with a positive response. Zasius states that Luther has had little success in resolving the problem but he has attained much popular support in that time for his cause. Zasius is a moderate and unwilling to speak out against the Catholic Church. Erasmus shares his humanist outlook and draws attention to the poor state of the Church which needs correction and like Zasius sees indulgences as one abuse of many. He does not mention Luther which is not surprising as they had fallen out by 1529 over the route to salvation. Erasmus does advocate the need for bishops to root out corruption but like Zasius he shows respect for Rome and is not radical to the point of speaking out against Papal authority. Yet here was one key reason for the success of Luther in the early years of the Reformation as the papacy was increasingly seen as an authoritative and greedy institution. Source E offers us another reason why Luther's ideas were popular, as it condemns the papacy with the phrase wicked fable that only the Pope can interpret the Bible and it can be argued that much of Luther's popularity was based upon the perceived weaknesses and abuses of the Catholic Church. Furthermore Luther's ideas spread rapidly and attracted support because his doctrine was a liberating one and put more emphasis upon the common man taking responsibility for his relationship with God. The reference in Source E to the priesthood of all believers highlights the point that by 1520 Luther's ideas had begun to take shape and had moved beyond mere opposition to indulgences.

In conclusion, the sources, apart from E which does not mention them, agree that Luther's attach on indulgences were a reason why he attracted support. The exploitation of German wealth by Rome struck a chord with his fellow Saxons. However, Luther was not the only person who voiced their objection to indulgences. There were others before him, such as Erasmus who had complained about the corruption which indulgences brought to the Church. This must mean that Luther attracted support not just because of his attitude to indulgences but because of some of his other ideas too. The sources mention Luther's objections to the role and power of the Pope which could also explain why he attracted support. This is particularly important when we consider whose support he attracted because of his attacks on the Pope, particularly Frederick the Wise. Frederick was no Lutheran but supported him because he objected to outside interference in Saxony from Rome. His support for Luther kept the Wittenberg reformer alive and allowed him to develop his ideas in relative safety.

Examiner's comments

The candidate uses the conclusion as a means of bolting on relevant own knowledge. This is ok but we prefer to see own knowledge integrated throughout the argument. Cassie should have saved the conclusion for a clear judgement on the question.

Examiner's overall comments

This is a good answer which uses all the sources to construct a relevant and balanced argument. It includes enough relevant own knowledge in the conclusion, although it would have been more effective if it had been integrated throughout the answer. This answer could also have been improved by being a little clearer and more explicit in its evaluation of source material and in showing how the provenance affects the tone and content of the sources.

GLOSSARY

Abuses should be seen as the corrupt practices of the Catholic clergy. An example of an abuse might be the buying or selling of a clerical post or title, a practice known as simony.

Anabaptists were more extreme Protestants who did not believe in infant baptism because they thought that the church should only include the 'godly' who were to be 'saved'. Thus they opted for what they called 'believer's baptism' which was undertaken when people were old enough to understand Anabaptist ideas. It should be pointed out that 'Anabaptists' was a term used by their opponents. They did not see themselves as re-baptisers.

Anticlericalism refers to criticism of the Catholic Church often based on the immoral actions of the Catholic clergy.

Apocalyptic message This is a message that predicts that the end of the world is coming soon.

Augustinian order In 587 St Augustine was sent to England to reform the Church of England. He set up a monastery in Canterbury and was chosen to be the first archbishop. The order that followed the rules of St Augustine is known as the Augustinians.

Catholic Mass The Mass refers to the prayers and ceremonies that make up the service of the Eucharist. It is important to recognise that the ordinary people might attend Mass on a regular basis but only take communion (or Eucharist) once a year. The Mass and Communion are the visible bond between people, priest, and bishop, who are all one body who share the one bread.

The **Curia** was the papal civil service or administrative unit.

Demagogue A leader of the people who attracts support through oratory.

Eucharist The Eucharist was a sacrament and miracle celebrating Christ's sacrifice and the Cross. The priest would consecrate the bread and wine at the altar, and they would then become the body and blood of Christ.

A **General Council of the Church** refers to the idea that leading archbishops and bishops from across Europe might meet to decide upon key doctrinal issues. The papacy never liked this idea as their authority would be undermined.

German New Testament Luther translated the New Testament from Greek (probably using the edition produced by Erasmus) into German between January and March 1522 while in Wartburg, although Luther continued to tinker with the translation until his death. With the mother tongue being increasingly used for church services across Germany, the need for such a translation was great, and the final result has been viewed as one of the most important contributions to German literature.

Hoc est corpus meum is the Latin for 'This is my body'. This term is at the heart of the Mass for, at this moment, the priest offers the bread as a symbol of Christ's body.

The **Holy Roman Empire** was a sprawling mass of over 400 separate states in central Europe, including Germany. Nominally, the **Holy Roman Emperor**, from the time of Charlemagne, had ruled over these states but, in reality, there was little centralisation. Each state had its own laws, customs and privileges. The emperor himself was elected by princes from the seven most powerful principalities: Saxony, Palatinate, Brandenburg, the King of Bohemia, Mainz, Trier and Cologne. These princes were known as electors.

The **Holy Scriptures** were the written word of God as outlined in the Old and New Testaments. For Christian humanists such as Erasmus, the problem with the Latin translations and the work of Church fathers such as Jerome, Origen and Augustine, was that they were deemed to be inaccurate and, over time, had been misinterpreted. Humanists spent much time editing New Testaments, translating and writing biblical commentaries. For reformers such as Luther, the words and substance of the scriptures became the crux of Protestant calls for reform.

The **Imperial Diet** was essentially the parliament of the Empire attended by princes and representatives of the imperial free cities. Imperial laws could be passed at the Diet.

Indulgences In the Catholic Church, the belief was that the Pope could issue a pardon for sins committed on earth that would mean that an individual would not have to serve time in purgatory for his or her sins. These pardons were called indulgences.

Legate A legate was a papal ambassador whose job it was to relate the views and policies of the Pope to foreign courts.

Lord's Supper Another term for Holy Communion. Both Luther and Zwingli rejected transubstantiation, yet whilst Luther believed in the real presence of Christ for the true believer, Zwingli saw the Lord's Supper as a purely symbolic service.

Magistrates are those who made up the ruling oligarchy of sixteenth-century towns.

Nuncios are representatives officially appointed by the Pope to convey decrees and legislation or just communicate with foreign kings in the role of ambassadors.

Ottoman Empire The most successful and powerful state in Europe between 1450 and 1600. Its navy controlled the Mediterranean, its army was formidable. The leader of the Empire between 1520 and 1566 was Suleiman the Magnificent. In 1529, he laid siege to the Habsburg capital Vienna, and in 1540 large parts of Hungary were annexed, thus proving that the Ottoman Empire was a constant threat to Charles.

Pacifist A pacifist is someone who believes in peace and is therefore opposed to violence or use of arms as a means of settling disputes.

Polygamy is the practice of having more than one wife at a time.

The pope in Rome The Catholic Church regards the pope as the successor of St Peter (head of the

Apostles) and, as such, he has full and supreme power of jurisdiction over the Church in matters of faith and discipline. Indeed, the pope is regarded as infallible on most matters of faith and morals. That is to say that any doctrinal decision he makes is binding on the whole Church. The pope is elected by a college of cardinals and sits at the top of a strict hierarchy consisting of cardinals, archbishops, bishops and priests. During the early modern period, the pope had great political power and influence, in part as a consequence of the Papal States in Italy over which he ruled.

Pragmatic is when something is done for reasons of common sense.

Preaching The purpose of Luther's sermons was to instruct the people in the new doctrine and to encourage them to support and follow the movement. Luther had thousands of his sermons published in order that travelling preachers could read his words aloud to the people. Most notable of Luther's sermons were the series of Christmas and Advent sermons published in 1522.

Primer A primer was a devotional book that included the psalms and the litany of saints. Dating back to the fourteenth century, primers were often seen as religious textbooks to teach and instruct children and adults alike.

Printing Fortunately for Luther he was able to make use of a relatively new invention, in the form of the printing press. The first press was put into production by Gutenberg in 1455 and by 1500 there were printing shops in over 60 German cities. The mass production of cheap pamphlets was crucial to the spread of Lutheranism.

To **recant** means that one no longer holds a certain opinion.

The **Renaissance** From the French meaning rebirth, the Renaissance is seen to centre around Italy, with the effects encompassing all of Europe. The period 1370–1527 is often deemed to be that in which literary and artistic talents such as Petrarch, Dante, Bruni and Boccaccio were allowed to flourish and a new wave of learning and thinking entered Europe. Whether such a period can actually be defined is a contentious issue, but the significance for the Reformation was that ancient, classical texts were re-evaluated and scripture re-translated. Also, Christian Humanism emerged from the literary and scholastic environment of the Renaissance.

Roods are replicas of the cross on which Jesus was crucified. Generally, roods were raised on a beam near the altar.

The Schmalkalden Articles, 1538 were written by Luther in 1537, published in 1538 and give us a clear insight into mature Lutheran doctrine and theology, as well as endorsing the use of force in defence of the gospel.

The Sixty-Seven Theses were a statement of Zwingli's doctrine intended for academic debate.

Transubstantiation is the Catholic belief that in the Mass, the bread and the wine were entirely transformed miraculously into the body and blood of Christ.

The Wittenberg Concord, 1536 rejoined the South German cities with the north through agreement over the Lord's Supper and an affirmation of the Augsburg Confession.

A **Woodcut** was a block of wood carved with a picture or design from which prints were made.

Zwickau Prophets were a group from Bohemia. Among their claims were the suggestions that they were in close communication with God, had no need of the Bible and that the ungodly should be slaughtered!

INDEX

Page numbers in italic refer to sources.

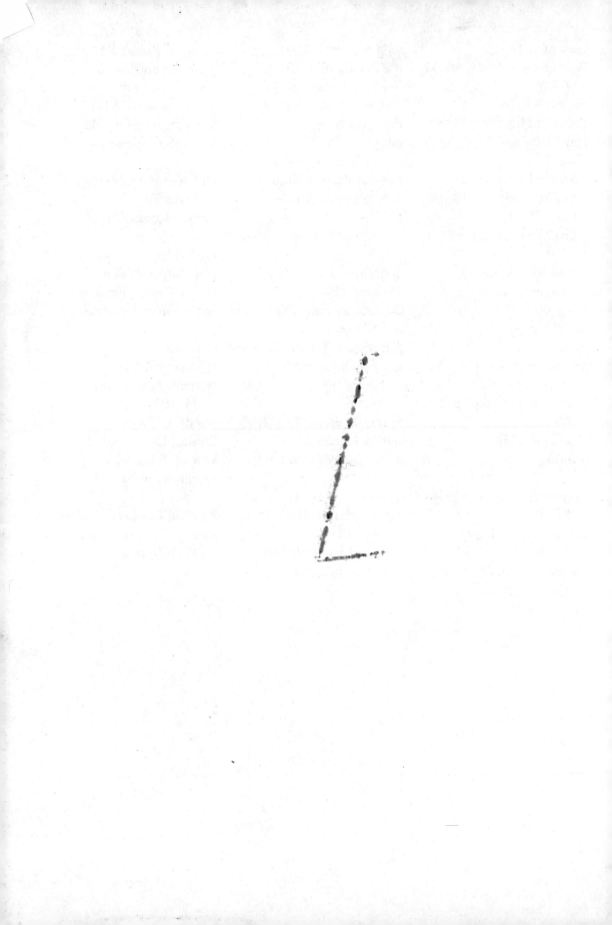